ONE EUROPE
100 NATIONS

CHANNEL VIEW BOOKS

An imprint of Multilingual Matters Ltd

Publishers of general and academic books,
journals and newletters in
multicultural and multilingual studies.

For details of our other publications, please contact:

Multilingual Matters Ltd,
Frankfurt Lodge,
Clevedon Hall,
Victoria Road,
Clevedon,
Avon BS21 7SJ,
England.

ONE EUROPE

100 NATIONS

Roy N. Pedersen

Foreword by Magnus Magnusson

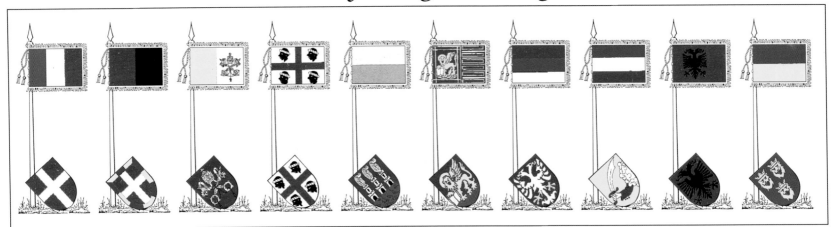

CHANNEL VIEW BOOKS

Clevedon – Philadelphia – Adelaide

Library of Congress Cataloging in Publication Data

Pedersen, Roy N. (Roy Norman)
One Europe — 100 Nations/Roy N. Pedersen
Foreword by Magnus Magnusson
p. cm
Includes bibliographical references
1. Europe — Politics and Government — 1989- 2. Europe — History —
Autonomy and Independence Movements. I. Title
D2009.P44   1992
940.55 — dc20

British Library Cataloguing in Publication Data

A CIP catalogue record for this book is available from the British Library.

ISBN 1-85359-123-8

CHANNEL VIEW BOOKS
An imprint of Multilingual Matters Ltd
UK: Frankfurt Lodge, Clevedon Hall, Victoria Road, Clevedon,
    Avon BS21 7SJ, England.
USA: 1900 Frost Road, Suite 101, Bristol, PA 19007, USA.
Australia: P.O. Box 6025, 83 Gilles Street, Adelaide, SA 5000, Australia.

Typeset by Photo-graphics, Honiton, Devon.
Printed and bound in Great Britain by WBC Print Ltd, Bridgend.

Contents

Foreword   6

Preface   7

Acknowledgements   8

Dedication   9

Introduction   10
  Unity and Diversity   10
  The European Spirit   11
  Many Tongues   11
  The Struggle for Democracy   12
  A Territorial Kaleidoscope   16
  The Heraldic Legacy   19
  The Flags   20
  The 100 Nations   20

Northern Enlightenment — The Scandinavian Lands   22

Britannia Overruled — The British Isles   31

The Low Countries — Benelux   41

Old Gaul — The French Lands   47

The Iberian Peninsula — Spain and Portugal   58

The Fatherland — Germany   68

Europe's Backbone — The Alpine Lands   89

Rome's Legacy — The Italian Peninsula   94

The Western Slavs — Poland and Czechoslovakia   103

The Byzantine Inheritance — South-East Europe   108

Soviet Transformation — The Former USSR in Europe   122

Variations on a Theme   133
  Eastern European Minorities   133
  Dispersed Minorities   133
  Nomadic Peoples   134
  The Division of Cyprus   134
  Alternative Developments   135

Towards a New Europe   137

Appendices
  1. The Family Tree of Europe's Languages   140
  2. Europe's Religious Spectrum   141
  3. The Persistence of Monarchy   141
  4. 1989: The Year of Revolution   142
  5. Independence Blossoms   143

Selected Bibliography   144

Foreword

Europe's 'hundred' nations have long and ancient pedigrees. Some became great imperial powers which sought to extinguish or marginalise the distinct identities of the other nations they came to dominate. This century has, however, witnessed the rebirth of a number of the smaller nations as one by one they have reasserted their independent place in the international family.

My own native Iceland, on the very edge of Europe, is a typical example. Its vigorously independent existence in Viking times was later reduced to near thralldom as a Danish possession for half a millenium. Over the last century a reawakened awareness of Iceland's rich heritage gave the Icelanders the confidence to seek and gain firstly, autonomy, then total independence as a modern and progressive nation state.

Although the Icelanders have been successful in throwing off foreign domination, they are equally conscious of the need to strengthen links with Europe as a whole. The Icelanders' prosperity, and perhaps their very existence, depends on striking the right balance — to be themselves while also enjoying the benefits, and shouldering the responsibilities, of being European.

This is indeed the great challenge for all Europeans in the last decade of the 20th century, nowhere more so than in rapidly changing Central and Eastern Europe. In *One Europe — 100 Nations*, Roy Pedersen explores the process and outlines the evolution of a new, unified, democratic European commonwealth of 100 free and equal nations.

Magnus Magnusson, 1992

Preface

All good men are international. Nearly all bad men are cosmopolitan. If we are to be international we must be national.

G. K. Chesterton

Europe's thirty-five old nation states have had their day. Yesterday's suppressed and undervalued peoples are stirring to create a new united European commonwealth within which 100 free nations can flower. The immense potential of this great commonwealth stems from the very diversity of Europe's peoples and institutions.

My work on *One Europe — 100 Nations* originated over twenty years ago. It stemmed from an interest in the development of the European Economic Community (EEC), as it was then called, and the simultaneous growth of home rule movements in Scotland, Wales and the other Celtic countries. This interest rapidly expanded to a study of the Scandinavian experience, then to Spain, and eventually to all Europe including the then mysterious Communist bloc.

The expansion of my geographical horizons kindled an intense fascination with the roots of national identity; ever recurring patterns were revealed and these struck chords in my own Scottish consciousness. Thus the historical foundations, the processes and power of linguistic and cultural revival, the heraldry and the national flags all became addictive fields of study.

This book is a distillation of that body of work, largely completed before the revolutionary events of 1989. Those events wholly vindicated the thesis that today's stateless nations, on both sides of the former 'Iron Curtain', are set fair to find cultural expression, linguistic freedom and political self-determination as part of the development of democracy itself. In other words to find their place as equals alongside their former oppressors.

Limits of space prevent all but a glimpse at each nation's story. To allow the text to flow and to avoid excessive repetition, each of these stories has where possible been given a different emphasis. But read as a whole, the resulting corpus of information and anecdote illustrates the wide variety of trends, situations and forces which are collectively at work in shaping the new unified but richly diverse Europe.

Maps, tables, historical data, information on all Europe's indigenous languages and minorities, together with full colour illustrations of the flags and arms of the new Europe's 'hundred' nations have been provided to help anchor the place of each nation, geographically, historically, linguistically and culturally in the greater European context.

One Europe — 100 Nations should not be read as an exact prediction. It illustrates rather an extrapolation from evidence that points to an unstoppable process of power redistribution fuelled by the collective aspirations of Europe's dispossessed peoples.

Roy N. Pedersen, 1992

Acknowledgements

An undertaking like *One Europe — 100 Nations* would not have been possible without the help and support of a large number of individuals and institutions. It is impossible to mention all who have over the years provided snippets of information, clues and contacts, but to every one the author's gratitude is extended.

Key information was kindly made available by the following institutions: the Baltic Council in London, CIEMEN in Barcelona, the European Bureau for Lesser Used Languages in Dublin, the Finnish Embassy in London, the Flag Research Center in Winchester, Mass., USA, the Goethe-Institut in London, and Xunta de Galicia in Santiago de Compostela, Galicia.

Warm thanks are extended to a host of individuals who sought and provided important data. Their number includes: Barbara Bird (Norway), Alberto Bistarelli (South Tyrol), Eugenio Busolini (Friuli), Mary Denovan (Scotland), Reidar Erke (Sapmi), Rob Gibson (Scotland), Andoni Gorostiaga (Euskadi), Roy Gronneberg (Shetland), Gosta Jellema (Friesland), Xavier Lamuela (Catalonia), Dr Finlay MacLeod (Scotland), Rebecah Muir (Portugal), Hans-Pavia Rosing (Greenland), Carme Fernandez Perez-Sanjulian (Galicia), Alem Surre-Garcia (Occitania), Maria Serena Tiella (Aosta), and Dr Whitney Smith (USA).

A special debt of gratitude is due to my Scottish friends and colleagues who read proofs and gave freely of their considered advice, support and time.

While every care has been taken to check sources and seek out errors, it is extremely difficult in a work of this breadth to be absolutely certain of total exactitude. Should any errors of fact or interpretation have crept in, these are the responsibility of the author alone.

Dedication

As my own work started, a small book emerged, unknown to me at the time, which neatly set out the philosophy, separately uncovered by myself in assembling *One Europe — 100 Nations*. That book, written in French, was called *L'Europe aux Cent Drapeaux* (Europe of a Hundred Flags). The author, Yann Fouère, described himself as a militant Breton, a militant federalist and militant European. He sought a single humane Europe, all of whose peoples were free.

To Yann Fouère's vision, I dedicate this book.

Introduction

UNITY AND DIVERSITY

A whirlwind of change is sweeping through Europe — a whirlwind born of two relentless trends — unity and diversity. Europe grows all the while more unified. In the West the European Community (EC) frees the movement of people, goods and services across frontiers. Eastern Europe moves headlong towards a more open and democratic way of living.

The 20th century has seen the fall one by one of the great European empires and a gradual process of decolonisation until, with unexpected suddenness, the last of the empires, the Soviet Union, has now disintegrated.

Such political change and the advance of technology, increasingly integrates hitherto separate and closed economies. Ever more powerful communications media make investment, mass production and distribution possible on an international scale.

At the same time, after years of suppression and attempted assimilation, national and linguistic minorities from Wales to Latvia and from the Ukraine to Brittany seek recognition of their rights to cultural expression and self determination. These small and undervalued peoples have discovered a new vigour which finds expression in a quite unexpected linguistic and cultural renaissance; in some cases of a quality capable of outshining the best efforts of the large states. The phenomenon has developed and grown through parallel concerns for art, the environment, human values, and a desire to conserve the best of the past.

This re-emergence of small nations in the face of gigantism may seem like paradox. It is not. The very strength which flows from the free movement of ideas now encourages the diversity of a hundred different European cultures to flower. As a Basque patriot put it, 'The more Basque I become, the more European I become also'. The very essence of Europe, and its greatness, stems from the diversity of its people.

The concept was anticipated in the 1930s by Scots writer, Neil Gunn, for whom the small nation had always been humanity's last bulwark for the individual against the machine. For him the small nation, with its concern for heritage and culture, created the intense vision and rebellion of the native spirit which internationalism subsequently enjoyed. In contrast he saw the uniformity of cosmopolitanism deadening creativity.

Each small nation has had to address the struggle for its own destiny in its own way. A feature of this current movement, however, is the growing mutual support and co-operation between and among such peoples internationally. Certainly this stems in part from the ease of modern travel and communication. But the driving force is a common purpose and spirit. That purpose is no longer merely to resist stagnation and decline; rather it is to create a climate in which previously marginalised cultures can grow once more.

In the European Community countries alone there are estimated to be more than 40 million people whose mother tongue is a 'lesser-used language', as distinct from the main language of the state in which they live. As confidence grows through contacts between these diverse peoples, so will their ability to achieve self-expression and self-determination. It now seems inevitable that a power shift away from large centralised states and closer to the people will be of such magnitude that the whole political and economic balance of Europe will be subject to a major readjustment. The process has already begun.

It is impossible to predict precisely how and when the new order will settle down but it is likely that small nations which have long been absorbed, suppressed and marginalised by the larger nation states will regain at least some measure of home rule. It is equally likely that Europe will become more integrated in terms of trade, monetary union and common standards. As part of this trend we may be surprised just how quickly new links are forged between Eastern and Western Europe across the now eroded 'Iron Curtain'.

The sun has set on the Europe of empires. A new dawn rises on a united Europe of a hundred free nations.

THE EUROPEAN SPIRIT

Each nation and ethnic group has its own identity, culture and collective beliefs, its own unique spirit. But there is undoubtedly also a pan European spirit of great strength and antiquity which through history has bound this diversity together.

The roots of European spiritually are pagan and lost in an unlettered tribal past. It is known that by the 4th century BC, Celtic tribes possessed great skill in metal work, astronomy and learning. They dominated much of Europe and eventually settled a vast tract spreading from what is now Portugal and the British Isles in the west to Asia Minor (modern Turkey) in the east. Although prone to internecine strife, these Celts developed advanced ideas of humanity including democracy, equality for women, protection of the sick and feeble, harmony with nature, love of art and self-expression, together with a communal and spiritual approach to life. The influence of the Celts on civilised European thought is greatly underestimated.

The well documented Greeks on the other hand gave respect for rationality and the autonomy of the individual. The Romans created the greatest system of organised power, law and order there had ever been. These contrasting traditions of civilised life met a new force which would come to dominate European thought and spirituality. That force was Christianity.

Christianity, which stems from the Jewish concept of a single god, was adopted in AD 324 by the Emperor Constantine as the state religion of the Roman Empire. Church and Empire became partners and the Church grew in strength even after the collapse of the Roman Empire in the west. In due course the Roman Church and the emerging Christian kingdoms became inter-twined. Bishops crowned kings and the Church as inheritor of Roman law laid down the rules and discipline of inter-state behaviour. Although the western Roman Empire had been swept away, the eastern Byzantine Empire based in Constantinople was to continue for many centuries, and with it the Church, but following the eastern Orthodox rather than western Roman tradition.

As these two traditions consolidated their influence throughout much of Europe, Islam emerged to threaten the Christian hegemony. By the early 8th century most of Spain had fallen to the Muslims. For the next 1000 years and more, European Christendom would strive to fend off succeeding waves of Islamic Moors, Mongols and Turks. Even today, when a secular and democratic way of life tends to overshadow religion, a resurgent Islam has served to emphasise and prompt a reappraisal of European values. In Appendix 2, the geographical disposition of Europe's religious spectrum is mapped.

The shared experience of the struggle to maintain and extend Christendom ultimately forged a consciousness of European identity on the medieval mind. This identity was underlined by the institutions of church, kingship, chivalry and heraldry, common to almost all the peoples in Europe, regardless of their ethnic origin or language.

MANY TONGUES

Language is fundamental to effective human organisation. It is also a key stimulus to the intellect and spirit. Well over 100 different languages and dialects are currently in use throughout Europe. They range from languages of empire like French, Spanish, English, German and Russian to unwritten dialects spoken by a few hundred people. Each of these languages and dialects embodies its own store of values — its own perspective on the world. This rich linguistic diversity is at the very heart of Europe's genius.

Languages have been classified into families. Nine out of ten Europeans speak languages which come within the Indo-European family. This in turn divides into branches, languages and dialects. The family relationships between the languages and the geographical extent of Europe's broad linguistic divisions are summarised in Appendix 1.

Many Europeans, especially ethnic minorities, are fluent in two or more languages. Such bilingual and multilingual people are privileged to view the world simultaneously through two or more windows. This not only broadens the individual's life experience and intellectual capacity but also fosters international understanding. Indeed monoglots (those who speak only one language) are increasingly regarded as linguistically and culturally disabled.

It is no longer acceptable for dominant majorities to suppress linguistic minorities. More and more the value of educating children through the medium of lesser-used mother tongues is recognised and encouraged by governments with surprisingly beneficial results. Self-confidence replaces apathy, growth replaces decline. Not all governments are yet so enlightened but the pressure for change is becoming irresistible. Modern methods and media facilitate language learning as never before. A multilingual future is undoubtedly a key to the new European renaissance.

Lest it be feared that linguistic pluralism on this scale could reduce Europe to an incomprehensible Babel, there is, as in other aspects of the evolving new Europe, a compensating factor: Euro-English, an international *lingua franca*, distilled from text-book usage in England and America and blended with advertising and pop jargon. Thus an Icelandic fish merchant will trade with a Spanish wholesaler through Euro-English; a Hungarian air traffic controller will give directions to a Dutch pilot in Euro-English.

This communication tool has little subtle idiom and generally has a 'continental' accent. For this reason, monoglot English speakers can have difficulty in being understood by Euro-English speakers through failure to adjust and simplify their 'register'. The English too must learn Euro-English!

The rapid growth of Euro-English provides the opportunity for all peoples to communicate internationally. It is, however, multilingualism which enables Europeans to enjoy, in their home territory, the richness of their own collective linguistic heritage and culture to the full.

The guarantee of linguistic and cultural protection is confirmed in a number of international agreements, including Article 27 of the United Nations Charter on Civil and Political Rights. In the 21st century linguistic and cultural self-determination, by small nations as well as large, will clearly be a vital element in enriching the diversity upon which Europe will thrive. It is the acceptable path to unity without the dulling effect of uniformity.

THE STRUGGLE FOR DEMOCRACY

Democratic government of the people by the people is not a new concept. It was practised instinctively by those flamboyant and artistic Celtic tribes who settled so much of Europe in the pre-Christian era. Democratic methods were developed by the Greeks and have cropped up from time to time and place to place throughout European history as a respected political principle.

The emergence of kings pursuing the concept of absolutism, backed by armed force and legitimised by a universal Church, was, however, not a favourable institutional structure for the development of democratic government. After all, the exploitation of the land for the gratification of dynastic ambition and personal enrichment, leaves little scope for relinquishing power to ordinary folk.

The Protestant Reformation of the 16th century was probably the first large-scale challenge to absolute power. It was not, however, until the 18th century and during the 'Age of Reason' that the concept of democracy gained sufficient credibility for it to stand a chance of implementation as a practical method of governance. Influential at the time were the writings and 'rabble rousing' of Thomas Paine, particularly his booklet *The Rights of Man*.

The outbreak of the Revolutionary War of the American colonists against the British led to the Declaration of Independence of 1776 and the eventual adoption of the Constitution of the United States of America. For the first time the principles of representative democracy were enshrined in the fabric of a nation state.

The world owes immense gratitude to the United States, not only for providing a viable demonstration model for the first modern democratic state, but for creating a workable 'federal' system allowing individual states considerable political autonomy within an overall framework set down for their collective benefit and co-operation.

In Europe the growth of the idea of democracy was causing much concern among the old monarchic order, which perceived a challenge to its privileged position of power. In 1789, when the Paris mob stormed the Bastille amid cries of 'Liberty, Equality, Fraternity', that challenge became real. Occurring as it did in the most powerful, prestigious and populous European state of the time, the French Revolution and its aftermath propagated radical ideas which were to dominate politics into the 20th century.

During the 19th century, as liberal concepts were gradually introduced in at least the more progressive countries, it is perhaps surprising that many of the old monarchies survived. If anything, by the end of the century, the royal houses attracted more popular support than ever before. Of course, the concept of absolutism had been discredited and royalty had, for the most part, learned to reach some form of accommodation with developing quasi-democratic assemblies or parliaments.

By the beginning of the 20th century the principle of universal suffrage was beginning to gain acceptability, for males at any rate. Apart from a few enlightened cases, female suffrage was to take some more decades before becoming common. Imperfect it may have been, but progress was real enough in that first optimistic decade of the new century. The old states and empires of Europe (mapped in Figure 1) were becoming 'constitutional' monarchies. A number of these survive to this day (see Appendix 3 for a summary of the current situation).

The comfortable old order was, however, swept away for ever by the Great War of 1914–18. In its aftermath, new and sinister forces of totalitarian Communism and Fascism emerged, fuelled by discontent caused through economic slump and depression. By the early 1940s, in the depths of the Second World War, liberal democratic processes were all but extinguished in Europe.

The productive capacity and economic clout of the United States of America saved democracy in Western Europe but left Central and Eastern Europe under Communist rule behind what by 1946 Churchill described as the 'Iron Curtain'. The ensuing 'cold war', 'arms race' and the creation in Europe of two opposing ideological, military and economic blocs, preoccupied political minds for nearly half a century.

In the post-war years Western Europe, with its evolving democratic structure, flourished under the protection of the North Atlantic Treaty Organisation (NATO). Eastern Europe, through the Warsaw Pact, presented a formidable military threat, but under a centralised authoritarian Communist system was unable to provide its people with the economic benefits they increasingly desired.

Several times efforts to seek liberty were crushed. In Hungary in 1956 Soviet Red Army tanks ruthlessly put down a popular uprising against Communist rule, as they did again to end the Czechoslovak 'Prague Spring' of 1968. Meanwhile, in 1961 the East German government built the infamous Berlin Wall in an attempt to stem the mass outflow of skilled emigrants discontented with the deficiencies of the Communist system.

FIG. 1 – THE OLD ORDER

'Europe of empires' as it was in the year 1900, shown relative to Europe's nation states as at the beginning of 1990.

1 Andorra	5 Denmark	9 Italy	13 Montenegro	17 Russian Empire	21 Sweden
2 Austro-Hungarian Empire	6 France	10 Liechtenstein	14 Netherlands	18 San Marino	22 Switzerland
3 Belgium	7 German Empire	11 Luxemburg	15 Portugal	19 Serbia	23 Ottoman Empire
4 British Empire (UK)	8 Greece	12 Monaco	16 Romania	20 Spain	

The latent craving for democracy and liberty could not be suppressed for ever. In 1980 Polish shipyard workers, under the leadership of Lech Walesa, challenged the monopoly of the Communist state's power by establishing the free trade union *Solidarity*. Although subsequently outlawed, *Solidarity* was eventually able to re-emerge as a major inspiration in the struggle for democracy throughout Eastern Europe.

The key to real change lay in the Soviet Union. In 1985 the new Soviet leader, Mikhail Gorbachev began a process which was to transform not only Eastern Europe but the quest for world peace. He set about the daunting task of shaking up the stagnating and corrupt Soviet system through two principles:

'*Glasnost*' (openness) encouraging free honest debate to challenge outdated ideas
and
'*Perestroika*' (restructuring), opening up the monolithic Soviet economy to market forces and modern decentralised management techniques.

In practice these principles were to stimulate a powerful demand for both democratisation in a general sense and for greater self-determination for many of the distinct non-Russian nationalities within the Soviet Union. In his external dealings, Gorbachev was instrumental in initiating a process of international arms reduction, making it clear that the Red Army would no longer intervene in the internal affairs of another country.

Then in 1989 the world watched on television, almost incredulously, as a breathtaking chain reaction of revolution swept through the Communist countries of Central and Eastern Europe. By the end of that astonishing year 'people power' had essentially driven totalitarian Communism from Europe. This ideological clear-out created new opportunities for the small and oppressed nations to seek their place as equals in the European family. The key events in '1989 — The Year of Revolution' are summarised in Appendix 4.

The following year featured the unification of East and West Germany and a series of open, democratic, multi-party elections throughout most of formerly Communist Central and Eastern Europe. This process was accompanied by large-scale withdrawals of Soviet troops. In the USSR and in Yugoslavia the advocates of democracy and independence were to face resistance from privileged conservatives in the Communist party and the army who sought to retain their power through the authority of a centralised state.

Matters came to a head in 1991 as Soviet and non-Serb Yugoslav republics openly committed themselves to independence during a period of worsening economic conditions exacerbated by world recession. The Communist-backed military attempted to reverse independence bids in the Baltic states, Slovenia and Croatia by force of arms. In Yugoslavia this intervention reached civil war proportions with heavy loss of life on both sides. Nevertheless, the resolve of the people of these nations to be free, backed by sympathetic world opinion, won the day for independence.

This struggle for democratic self-determination in Central and Eastern Europe brought about the most rapid and radical change in the geopolitics of the region since the end of the First World War. Within two years, fourteen new states declared independence (see Appendix 5). The courage and success with which these bids for freedom were made served as an inspiration and example to those nations in Western Europe who also sought autonomy or independence.

In 1992, for the first time, opinion polls showed over 50% of Scots in favour of full independence, with 80% in favour of some form of home rule. In Wales, a renewed interest in political autonomy also became manifest. Democracy and independence have become natural partners.

This struggle for democratic self-determination by the non-Russian Soviet republics served as an inspiration and example to those nations in Western Europe who also sought autonomy or independence.

A TERRITORIAL KALEIDOSCOPE

Throughout history Europe's kingdoms and principalities have formed an ever-changing pattern. In the 20th century alone two world wars saw major re-drawing of the European map, with, for example, the disappearance of the once mighty Austro-Hungarian Empire and the creation of Poland, Czechoslovakia, Yugoslavia and numerous other changes. Between 1945 and 1990, however, the borders of Europe's 35 nation states (see Figure 2) remained virtually unaltered.

On the evidence of history such a circumstance could not last. The static map masked a pent-up undercurrent of change. Yesterday's rigid institutions, political structures and nation states are no longer appropriate for tomorrow. In the complex modern world the concept of total national sovereignty is no longer a tenable one, even for super-powers. All states are now interdependent.

Pollution, for example, a major public concern, respects no frontiers. It is a supra-national issue which requires supra-national measures to control. The same is increasingly true of finance, trade, broadcasting, industrial production, terrorism, narcotics dealing, tourism, the arts, defence, air transport . . . and the list is growing. Only the emerging network of supra-national institutions with the backing and authority of a genuinely pan-European regime of cooperation can effectively handle all these issues.

Just as even the largest European states can no longer cope alone with issues which have assumed a supra-national dimension, so are they also less able to satisfy the growing aspirations of their ethnic and linguistic minorities and the populations of absorbed territories which have a memory of former independence. The balance has therefore shifted in favour of self-determination for these 'stateless nations'. They themselves, rather than some distant central authority, generally know best how to address their own problems and development needs.

Progress towards self-determination varies from case to case. In Germany for example, each *Land* has already a large measure of autonomy within an overall federal structure, similar to the position of the individual states within the United States of America. France on the other hand, is by tradition highly centralised and, despite pressure, has so far conceded little real recognition of long-standing minority aspirations. Real change has occurred in Denmark, whose Faroe Islands and Greenland territories have achieved home rule with the constructive support of the Danish government. In the late 70s, the Basques, Catalans and Galicians gained varying degrees of autonomy from the formerly centralist Spanish government. In the Soviet Union and Yugoslavia, with the collapse of Communism, autonomy, independence and linguistic rights for non-Russians and non-Serbs have become a reality. Elsewhere in Europe also radical change is in the air.

With growing interdependence on the one hand and emerging self-determination on the other, the distinction between nation states and stateless nations starts to blur and lose its significance. An almost automatic consequence of these complementary trends is that as the large states lose their ideocracy, purpose, and therefore their dominance, the stateless nations, with their strong sense of historical or ethnic cohesion, are emerging as autonomous or independent political units.

The process is bound to be volatile, particularly as such re-alignments tend to take place over a short historical timespan. Of course nobody can predict precisely how such a radical power shift will work out in practice. It is possible however, by interpreting current trends and aspirations, to create a model which identifies a feasible future pattern of European self-governing territories. Each of them has some, if not all, of the following characteristics:

- existing statehood or a history of former statehood;
- a distinct culture or religion;
- a distinct language or dialect;
- the existence of a popular movement for autonomy or independence;
- geographical distinctiveness.

FIG. 2 – EUROPE'S 'COLD WAR' NATION STATES

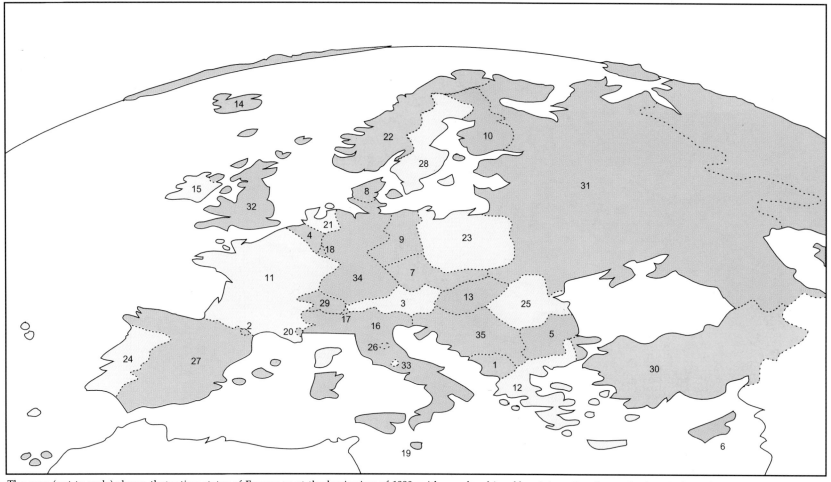

The map (not to scale) shows the nation states of Europe as at the beginning of 1990, with membership of key international organisations indicated. The letters in brackets ( ) are the national distinguishing signs for use on motor vehicles in international traffic.

1 Albania (AL)
2 Andorra (AND)
3 Austria (A)[3]
4 Belgium (B)[2]
5 Bulgaria (BG)[1]

6 Cyprus (CY)
7 Czechoslovakia (CS)[1]
8 Denmark (DK)[2]
9 East Germany (DDR)[1]
10 Finland (SF)[3]

11 France (F)[2]
12 Greece (GR)[2]
13 Hungary (H)[1]
14 Iceland (I)[3]
15 Ireland (IRL)[2]

16 Italy (I)[2]
17 Liechtenstein (FL)
18 Luxemburg (L)[2]
19 Malta (M)
20 Monaco (MC)

21 Netherlands (NL)[2]
22 Norway (N)[3]
23 Poland (PL)[1]
24 Portugal (P)[2]
25 Romania (RO)[1]

26 San Marino (RSM)
27 Spain (E)[2]
28 Sweden (S)[3]
29 Switzerland (CH)[3]
30 Turkey (TR)

31 USSR (SU)[1]
32 UK (GB)[2]
33 Vatican (V)
34 West Germany (D)[2]
35 Yugoslavia (YU)

1. Member of the Council for Mutual Economic Aid (COMECON)   2. Member of the European Community (EC)   3. Member of the European Free Trade Association (EFTA)

17

FIG. 3 – EUROPE'S HUNDRED NATIONS

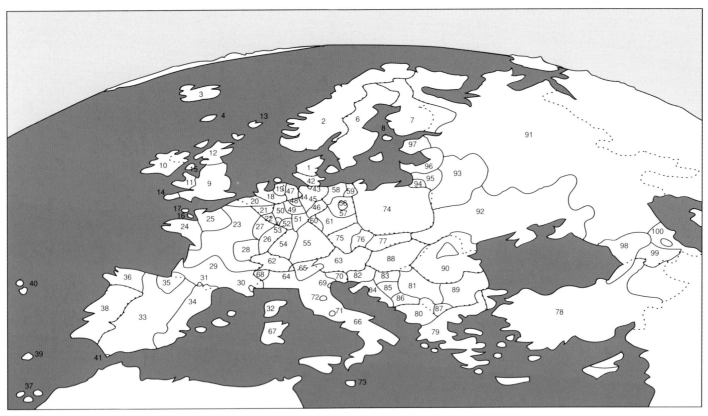

70 Friuli
71 Vatican
72 San Marino
73 Malta

WESTERN SLAVS

74 Poland
75 Bohemia
76 Moravia
77 Slovakia

SOUTH-EAST EUROPE

78 Turkey
79 Greece
80 Albania
81 Serbia
82 Slovenia
83 Croatia
84 Dalmatia
85 Bosnia Hercegovina
86 Montenegro
87 Macedonia
88 Hungary
89 Bulgaria
90 Romania

FORMER USSR

91 Russia
92 Ukraine
93 Belarus
94 East Prussia
95 Lithuania
96 Latvia
97 Estonia
98 Georgia
99 Armenia
100 Azerbaijan

The 100 nations are
shown relative to
Europe's nation
states as at the
beginning of 1990.

SCANDINAVIA

1 Denmark
2 Norway
3 Iceland
4 Faroes
5 Greenland
6 Sweden
7 Finland
8 Åland Islands

THE BRITISH ISLES

9 England
10 Ireland

11 Wales
12 Scotland
13 Shetland
14 Cornwall
15 Isle of Man
16 Jersey
17 Guernsey

LOW COUNTRIES

18 Netherlands
19 Friesland
20 Flanders
21 Wallonia
22 Luxemburg

FRENCH LANDS

23 France
24 Brittany
25 Normandy
26 Alsace
27 Lorraine
28 Burgundy
29 Occitania
30 Monaco
31 Andorra
32 Corsica

IBERIA

33 Castille

34 Catalonia
35 Euskadi
36 Galicia
37 Canary Islands
38 Portugal
39 Madeira
40 Azores
41 Gibraltar

GERMANY

42 Schleswig Holstein
43 Hamburg
44 Bremen
45 Hanover

46 Brunswick Lüneburg
47 Oldenburg
48 Schaumberg-Lippe
49 Westphalia
50 Rhineland
51 Hesse
52 Palatinate
53 Saarland
54 Swabia
55 Bavaria
56 Berlin
57 Brandenburg
58 Mecklenburg
59 Pomerania

60 Thuringia
61 Saxony

ALPINE LANDS

62 Switzerland
63 Austria
64 Liechtenstein
65 Tyrol

ITALIAN LANDS

66 Italy
67 Sardinia
68 Aosta
69 Venice

The resulting list of territories, one hundred in number, is set out in Figure 3 with a map to show their location. Each is described separately in the body of this book.

Of these '100 nations', the average population per territory works out at about six million. It is of interest that this equates quite closely with the average population of individual US states. In Europe however the size will vary enormously from a few thousand people in each of the 'micro states' to over 100 million in European Russia. This size differential is another expression of Europe's rich diversity.

The development of nations is tied up in language, culture, history, politics and territory. National identity is powerfully reinforced by symbols. Within the European tradition, heraldry and flags form a universal system of national symbolism which focus and distinguish national identities. Their place in the re-emergence of Europe's nations is described in the following pages.

THE HERALDIC LEGACY

In 1095 Christendom was called to arms to liberate the Holy Land from the expansion of Islam: so began the first crusade. Such a large body of men from all over Europe, working for a common cause but speaking diverse tongues and unrecognisable to even their own countrymen due to heavy armour cladding, required a means of ready identification. Decoration of their equipment (helmets and shields in particular) by use of simple designs in clear contrasting colours was the solution. This is the origin of heraldry — a means of distinguishing warrior from warrior.

By the end of the 12th century a set of rules had evolved which governed the practice of heraldry throughout most of Christian Europe. The principal element in a coat of arms is the shield divided according to strict rules or decorated with a motif or motifs (charges). Above the shield can be placed a helmet with crown or coronet (in the case of kings, princes and higher nobility), crest and mantling (originally cloth fastened to the helmet and hanging over the wearer's shoulders to protect him from the sun). Some coats of arms may also be portrayed with 'supporters' (animals, fabulous creatures or humans) which may stand on a 'base' (or compartment), a plinth or motto scroll.

Only the shield is essential. A strict rule of heraldry is that a metal (gold or silver) should not be superimposed on another metal, nor should a tincture (colour) be superimposed on another tincture. Metal should therefore be on tincture or tincture on metal. This is the single secret of the dramatic impact and power of heraldry. Other rules govern the divisions of the shield and tradition largely governs possible charges. The number of variations is almost infinite but generally speaking the simpler the design, the older the arms.

In due course arms became hereditary and controlled by kings. With the extinction and amalgamation of old royal lines and decline of monarchy generally, the original royal arms have evolved as national rather than personal insignia. Even in some countries when under Communist rule, like Poland and Czechoslovakia, the ancient royal arms continued in uninterrupted official use as the emblems of state. In 1989 Hungary, the Baltic states and other Soviet republics re-adopted their old arms formerly suppressed by the Communists as another step in the process of re-establishing cultural roots.

Heraldry is not just used by governments. Bearing in mind its medieval origins and the obsolescence of its original purpose, it is quite remarkable how commonly heraldry is used as a popular statement of national identity. It is found in the form of vinyl stickers on cars and trucks, sew-on badges on backpacks, and marketing logos on beers, wines and spirits, tourist brochures, official publications and in many other manifestations.

Coats of arms have been found to exist for each of the hundred nations identified in the previous chapter. The majority are of great antiquity, simplicity and beauty, reflecting the complex warp and weft of medieval dynastic relationships. As a political force the dynasties have become redundant, or of little more than symbolic significance. The heraldry remains, and it springs from the very roots of the European tradition. Heraldry is a key ingredient in the symbolic mortar which binds Europe's diverse nations into a single family.

THE FLAGS

The flag represents, as no other material symbol can, the common bond among the people of a nation. It represents status, history, loyalty and future purpose. It is colourful and dramatic. The flag has immense power because it is a physical object which transcends the intellect and connects directly with the spirit.

All states have flags. The use of flags, or flag-like vexilloids, reaches back into the mists of time. National flags like the Scottish Saltire and the Danish Danneborg have very long pedigrees. The origin of most national flags, however, is historically recent. In fact the general adoption of national flags did not evolve until the 18th century. Hitherto flags had been regarded as symbols of the authority of the monarch or state rather than of the people.

The French Revolution brought about a change in attitudè, as did the 'romantic movement' of the 19th century, whereby the flag became a popular symbol or rallying point for the common people in the struggle against their oppressors. In this way, as countries gained autonomy or independence, the 'rebel' flag, or some variant of it, has frequently become adopted as the official national flag of the new state or autonomous territory.

The process is still very much underway especially in the USSR, where the various republics' traditional flags, long suppressed by the Communist authorities, have re-emerged as popular expressions of national identity. These flags, used by the formerly independent countries, have now been officially readopted to replace the sterile 'differenced' variants of the USSR hammer and sickle flag created in the 1950s.

In other Eastern European countries too, flags featured prominently in the revolutionary activities of 1989. A particularly dramatic gesture in both Hungary and Romania was the tearing out of the unpopular Communist emblems from the centres of the otherwise traditional flags of these countries, leaving a hole to symbolise very graphically the intended change of regime.

Including the currently stateless nations, a recognised flag exists for all 100 nations described in this book. Each is illustrated together with the appropriate arms adjacent to the relevant textual description. One page is set aside for each nation.

In many cases the designs of flags and arms have varied over time; reflecting different regimes, dynasties or alliances. The versions illustrated represent the author's interpretation of appropriate future usage, which, so far as is practical, selects the simplest, and generally most striking, acceptable designs, consistent with historical precedent. There are some cases in which bi-colour and tricolour are shared by more than one nation. Where it is necessary to make a distinction, this can be done by adding the appropriate shield (see, for example, Lorraine). The plain flag may still be used locally.

Colour rendition is as close to actual specification as can be achieved within the limits of the graphic and printing methods used. Many of the flags and arms illustrated are currently officially authorised by governments. Others, as yet, are not.

With their bold economical designs and bright colours, these flags collectively offer the new Europe a coherent system of national symbolism which has powerful dramatic presence and is rooted in popular tradition.

THE 100 NATIONS

The pages which follow set out a brief description of the origin, history, minorities, linguistic struggle, political status and other details as appropriate for each of Europe's hundred potentially or *de facto* self-governing nations. In addition, the appropriate flag and arms for each nation are illustrated and a note on their origin and usage provided.

The nations are grouped geographically with an introductory background note for every group, starting in the north west with the Scandinavian lands, and finishing in the east with the European nations of the former USSR.

As space is limited to one page per nation, the current (and where relevant prospective) political status of each nation is summarised in cryptic form according to the following key:

Political Status

A An autonomous state or region under the control of another state but with a measure of democratic self-government.

C A central dominant state exercising political control over another nation or other nations.

D A dependent nation or territory with little or no autonomy and incorporated within another state.

I An independent state with full self-government.

Future Prospect

> With a prospect of change in status to . . .

[>] May but unlikely to change status to . . .

Qualifications

f Existing within a federal system.

m Involving a merger of two or more territories.

r With reduced area of political control.

? Status in dispute.

The figure 2 or 3 indicates number of territories.

Substitution of the appropriate phrase indicated above for the successive letter(s) or symbol(s) shown against each nation reveals its current and prospective political status. The system is illustrated by the following examples:

Norway – I   An independent state (no prospect of change).

Wales – D > A or I   A dependent nation with little or no autonomy incorporated within another state (the UK), with a prospect of change in status to an autonomous state under the control of another state but with a measure of self-government, or to an independent state with full self-government.

Catalonia – 3A & D > Im   Three autonomous regions under the control of another state (Spain) with a measure of self-government, and a dependent territory with no political autonomy and incorporated within another state (France), all with the prospect of becoming a (single) independent state involving a merger of (the above) territories.

As a cryptic method of conveying information, the formula is necessarily 'broad brush'. It ignores the subtleties of individual cases, but amplification is included within the actual text covering the nation concerned.

It has to be said that the prognosis for change in political status of any nation is highly conjectural and can only be based on subjective judgement, taking into account past processes of development elsewhere, current political, cultural, and linguistic activity, and cyclical changes in national and international mood. It would be very surprising if events were to evolve exactly as set out in this book; strong grounds do, however, exist for believing that as Europe becomes more unified, there will be a major political power shift in favour of many of the smaller nations described in the pages which follow.

One thing is certain, after almost half a century of virtual *status quo*, big changes are under way among Europe's 100 nations. Only time itself will reveal how the drama unfolds but the following pages set the scene.

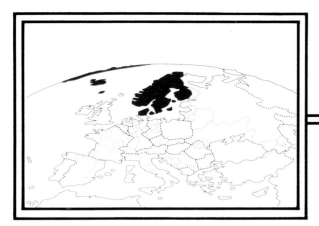

1 Denmark 2 Norway 3 Iceland
4 Faroes 5 Greenland 6 Sweden
7 Finland 8 Åland Islands

Northern Enlightenment
THE SCANDINAVIAN LANDS

The group of countries which occupy the northwestern portion of Europe share a heritage which has created a common Scandinavian culture. This sharing of ideas and experiences predates the founding of the three ancient kingdoms of Denmark, Norway and Sweden, whose boundaries have ebbed and flowed over each other's territory for the last 1000 years.

The vigour and enterprise of the Scandinavian Vikings between the 8th and 12th centuries led to the creation of a trading network which penetrated the further extremities of Europe. They even established a precarious and temporary toehold in North America, 400 years before Columbus.

Colonisation followed trade. The Scandinavian settlements in the British Isles, Normandy and Russia were subsequently absorbed by other cultures. Scandinavian influence in Finland and Greenland remains strong. In the Faroe Islands, Iceland and Åland it is total. In the 20th century, the Scandinavians have been pioneers in devolving home rule to dependent territories.

Today the Scandinavian peoples are noted for a highly developed sense of democracy and impartiality, coupled with a broad world outlook. Their material standard of living is among the world's highest, with extensive social welfare provisions. In many other respects the Scandinavian states are models to which many smaller nations aspire.

The eight Scandinavian nations have formed a supra-national organisation called the Nordic Council which promotes Scandinavian culture and mutual co-operation.

DENMARK

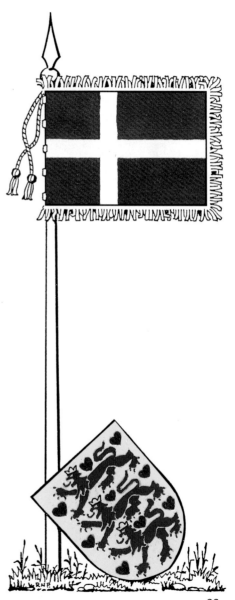

A monarchy with the oldest dynasty in Europe and the oldest national flag used by a current nation state makes Denmark an appropriate place from which to begin the story of the changing fortunes of Europe's nations.

Small but fertile, Denmark was in the Middle Ages the centre of a large territory which at various times included England, Norway, Greenland, Iceland, Sweden, Finland and a number of North German and Baltic lands. England and Sweden regained their independence at an early date. Norway was lost to Sweden in 1814 following the Napoleonic War. This left Denmark with the former Norwegian Atlantic possessions of the Faroe Islands, Iceland and Greenland.

As a consequence of pressure for home rule in the 20th century, Denmark has granted increasing autonomy (and total independence in the case of Iceland) to these territories.

Today Denmark, an EC member, is a prosperous and modern democratic state which successfully combines pride of tradition with a broad world outlook. There is a small German minority with protected linguistic rights.

The coat of arms of three blue lions among red hearts (formerly water lilies) on a gold shield dating from Knud IV, c. 1190) has been in continuous use since that time. The flag — the 'Danneborg' — is said to have dropped from heaven in 1219 turning defeat into victory for the Danish crusaders in the Battle of Lindanaes.

C > Cr

NORWAY

The bold exploits of the Norwegian Vikings are legendary. One of their number, Harold Fairhair, unified Norway in 872.

In 1319 the Norwegian royal house became extinct and King Magnus of Sweden succeeded to the throne. In 1397 the country became a Danish possession. Norway suffered terribly from the Black Death and also from exploitation by German *Hanse* merchants.

Literary life declined. The language used by the bourgeoisie became more and more influenced by Danish whereas the vernacular of the common folk remained closer to Old Norse.

In 1814 Denmark, which had supported Napoleon, was made to transfer Norway to Sweden. The Norwegians resented this and throughout the 19th century writers and artists led a process to Norwegianise the language and national consciousness.

Language development followed two separate strands. One sought gradually to Norwegianise Danish. This evolved into a form of Norwegian known as *'Riksmal'*. The other, assembled from the more conservative western dialects, became known as *'Landsmal'*. As both these forms evolve, they are being encouraged to converge into a common Norwegian language. A third language is that of the Sami (Lapp) people of northern Norway. In recent decades they have gained official recognition and protection on an international basis.

It was not until 1905 that Norway achieved independence from Sweden. Since then the Norwegians have prospered.

The Norwegian arms date from the end of the 12th century. The flag dates from 1821 and was officially acknowledged in 1898.

ICELAND

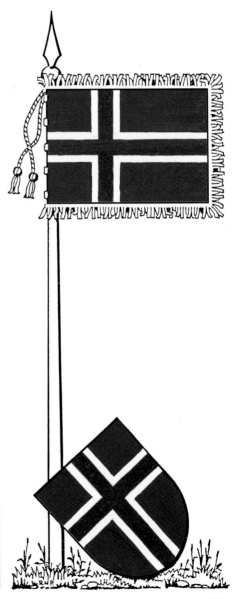

The 'Land of Ice and Fire' was originally discovered by Irish monks in the 7th century. The first Viking settler, according to the *'Landnama-bok'*, was a Norwegian chieftain, Ingolfur Arnarson, who reached the shores of Iceland in 874. Three years later he made his permanent home at Reykjavik which in due time emerged as Iceland's capital.

The enterprising Norsemen quickly colonised this rugged virgin land. In 930 they established the Althing, one of the world's oldest surviving parliaments. From Iceland the intrepid Vikings sent expeditions to Greenland and the North American mainland but it was only in Iceland that a permanent Scandinavian settlement survived. It thrived and produced a classical saga literature incorporating Old Norse values which has become an important ingredient in European civilisation.

Iceland lost her independence to Norway in 1262 and then to Denmark in 1380. This reduced the nation's fortunes for some 500 years. The 19th century, however, saw a national revival.

In 1874 the Danish king granted Iceland a separate constitution with a small measure of self-government. Home rule was granted in 1904, independence in personal union with Denmark in 1918, and in 1944 the new Republic of Iceland was established after 678 years of foreign rule. The Icelandic language is the closest of the Scandinavian languages to the Old Norse of the Vikings.

The Icelandic flag originated around 1913 and became official in 1915 for use by Icelandic ships. The old arms of Iceland, from the 15th century, was a silver stockfish beneath a gold crown on a red field. The shield of the present arms repeats the design of the flag and was adopted in 1919.

THE FAROE ISLANDS

'The Sheep Islands' lie isolated in the Atlantic 575 km west of Norway, midway between Shetland and Iceland. The first inhabitants were Irish hermit monks who around AD 700 were attracted by the remoteness of this dramatically beautiful land. The monks were displaced in about AD 800 by Viking settlers from whom the present inhabitants are largely descended.

A Norwegian dependency until the 14th century, the Faroe Islands passed with Norway to the Danish Crown in 1380. When Norway was ceded to Sweden under the Peace of Kiel in 1814, the Faroes remained with Denmark, along with Iceland and Greenland.

Although the question of self-government had arisen from time to time, the Faroes remained an administrative province (*amt*) of Denmark until the Second World War when metropolitan Denmark and the Faroes found themselves occupied by opposing sides. The Faroes had to fend for themselves (under allied occupation) for the five war years. As a result of the demands put forward at the end of the war the Faroes were made a self-governing nation under the Danish crown. The economy was thereby transformed to one of the most affluent in Europe.

The Faroese language, closely related to Icelandic, was a decaying and unwritten patois by the 19th century. It has been saved and has now fully replaced Danish as the official and *de facto* language in all spheres of Faroese life.

The arms are traditional, representing the old wool economy of the islands. The flag, designed by Faroese students in 1919, was first used officially in 1940, under decree of the British occupying forces, to distinguish Faroese ships from (enemy) Danish vessels. It has been the national flag since 1948.

GREENLAND

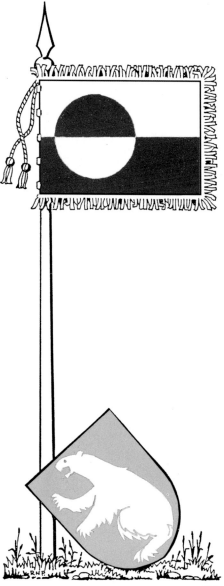

This vast Arctic land was first sighted by a European in about AD 900, when an Icelandic Viking en route from Norway was blown off course by storms. Iceland itself had only been settled two generations before. In 982 an Icelander, Eric the Red, was banished, and recalling the report of land to the west, set out to explore it. On his return to Iceland in 985 he enticed settlers to join him in the land he called 'Greenland'.

'The Saga of the Greenlanders' and 'Eric the Red's Saga' tell of these adventures and the Viking colonisation of Greenland, which lasted 500 years. Eric's son Leif had the joint distinction of introducing Christianity to the colony and discovering Vinland (America), which was also settled for a brief period.

After about 1350 contact between Greenland and Europe had become intermittent. Meanwhile deteriorating climate and marauding Eskimos rendered the colony extinct by around 1500. In 1721 the Danish government sent an expedition to search for traces of the vanished Scandinavian settlements. The farms and churches were deserted.

A new European (Danish) colony was created and integrated within the Kingdom of Denmark. Since 1979 the 54,000 Greenlanders, mainly Inuit (formerly called Eskimos), have enjoyed home rule. Whilst Danish remains in administrative use, the Inuit language is now increasingly used in most spheres.

The new flag of Kalatdlit Nunat (land of the Greenlanders), adopted on 21st June 1985 represents the sun rising over the Arctic ice and the red and white of Denmark. The use of 'the Greenlandic bear' as an armorial device is first recorded in 1666 and remains in official use today.

SWEDEN

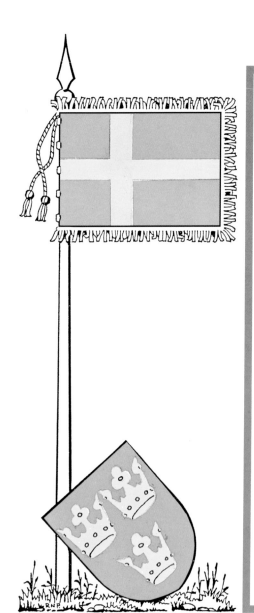

The Swedes have inhabited Scandinavia since pre-historic times. Tacitus, in AD 98, described the Sviones as 'mighty in ships and arms'. The realms of the Swedes and their neighbours, the Goths, were united around the year 600 to form the kingdom of Sweden, making it of more ancient foundation than any other major nation state in Western Europe.

During the Viking period (AD 800–1050) the Scandinavians were masters of the European seas, undertaking aggressive commercial expeditions to the furthest parts of the known world. While the Danes and Norwegians ventured west the Swedish Vikings pushed east and south to the Orient and Byzantium. In the process they founded, at Novgorod, a state that later was to become a component of the mighty realm of Russia.

Sweden was slow to put aside paganism but by 1160 was sufficiently Christian to conduct a crusade against Finland which was thereafter incorporated into Sweden for 650 years. From 1389 Sweden was in union with Denmark/Norway until 1521 when Gustavus Vasa re-established the independent Swedish throne. His forty-year rule saw the creation of the modern Swedish state which became a great European power in the 17th century.

Sweden lost Finland to Russia as a consequence of the Napoleonic Wars but gained Norway from Denmark. From that time Sweden has enjoyed a period of peaceful neutrality. The union with Norway was dissolved peaceably in 1905. The Swedish language remains universally spoken. There are small Finnish and Sami (Lapp) minorities.

The three crowns have been an emblem of Sweden since 1364 and the flag can be traced back to about 1500.

I

FINLAND

Related to the Estonians, and more distantly to the Hungarians, but unrelated to the mainstream Indo-European peoples of Europe, the Finns had migrated to Finland from the Urals and the Volga by the 8th century, driving the indigenous Sami (Lapps) northwards.

In 1154 the Swedish crusades forcibly converted the pagan Finns to Christianity and established Swedish rule in Finland. In 1362 Finland became an administrative province of Sweden. During the Napoleonic Wars, after five and a half centuries of Swedish rule, Finland passed to Russia and suffered intense Russification.

A national reawakening gathered momentum in the 19th century, as in many other countries. With it came demands for official recognition of the suppressed Finnish language. Activists placed much emphasis on developing a sense of national pride through a new Finnish-medium school system. Official status for Finnish was gained in 1902.

With the Russian revolution and the end of the First World War, Finland achieved full independence in 1917. The majority language today is Finnish, although there are also Swedish and Sami minorities. There are Finnish minorities in Sweden and the USSR. Soviet Finns seek re-incorporation within Finland.

Today Finland is a prosperous democratic state whose neutral status allows it to act as a bridge between East and West.

The arms of Finland have been in use since the 1580s, the scimitar trod underfoot by the lion representing danger from the East. The roses are for the nine traditional provinces of Finland. The flag, of Scandinavian pattern, proposed by the poet Zakarias Topelius, was adopted after independence.

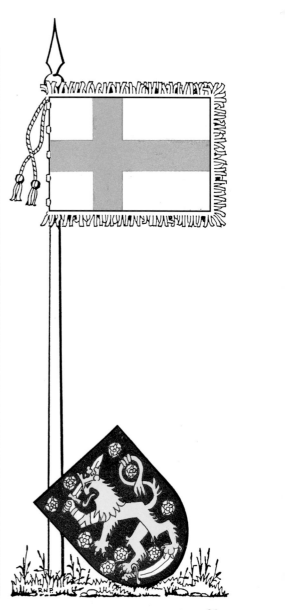

ÅLAND ISLANDS

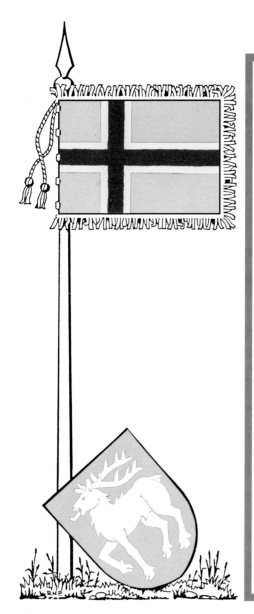

The Swedish-speaking population of this Baltic archipelago, mid way between Sweden and Finland, have found themselves successively under Swedish, Russian and Finnish control. In the mid 19th century motives of political security led the 'Great Powers' to declare the island a demilitarised zone. This status has lasted through both World Wars until the present day.

With the creation of the Finnish state at the end of the First World War a dispute with Sweden on the national status of the Åland Islands was settled by the League of Nations in Geneva in 1921: Åland became an autonomous Swedish-speaking province of the Republic of Finland.

This autonomy has developed substantially over the years and has provided a model for the introduction of regional autonomy elsewhere — e.g. the Faroe Islands, Spain etc. In general, the efforts made by Ålanders around 1920 for reunion with Sweden have long been replaced by a strong desire of the islanders to govern themselves.

Dating from the early 17th century, the arms of the Åland Islands show a hart (stag) on a blue field. The flag originates in the 1920s and was officially adopted in 1954.

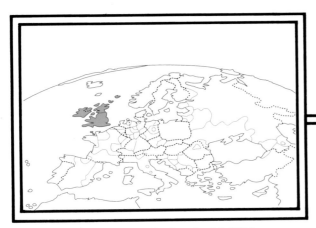

9 England   10 Ireland   11 Wales
12 Scotland   13 Shetland
14 Cornwall   15 Isle of Man
16 Jersey   17 Guernsey

Britannia Overruled
THE BRITISH ISLES

While partly under Roman administration during the early centuries of the first millennium AD, Great Britain, Ireland, and well over 100 smaller islands, which altogether form the British Isles, were inhabited by peoples of Celtic race and language.

When the legions left, as the Roman Empire imploded in the 5th century, the eastern shore lay open to pagan sea-borne Germanic invaders. These Angles, Saxons and Jutes landed and settled in increasing numbers, coalescing into a new English people. The more cultured Celtic Britons presented a long and hard-fought resistance but found themselves pushed further and further west. Their descendants are the Welsh and Cornish of today.

Ireland, like Scotland, had remained outside the Roman Empire. Around the time of the Anglo-Saxon invasion of England the Gaels of Ireland, a Celtic people distinct from the Britons, expanded their territory into south-west Scotland. By the 12th century Gaelic was the vernacular and court language of most of Scotland, the Isle of Man, and all Ireland.

The subsequent history of the British Isles has featured the often tense relationship between Anglo-Saxon England and her Celtic neighbours. In 1801, for the first time, all the nations of the British Isles were ruled from London as one 'United Kingdom', which in turn became the hub of the British Empire.

This once mighty structure began to disintegrate with the secession of much of Ireland in 1919, and the granting of self-government to most of the overseas possessions by the 1960s.

31

ENGLAND

Anglo-Saxon unity was first successfully encouraged by Alfred the Great, King of Wessex, who organised resistance to the Viking Danes. At that time Danes occupied most of northern England. Eventually the English nation emerged as an amalgam of Anglo-Saxon and Dane.

As a result of a disputed succession after the death of King Edward (the Confessor), William Duke of Normandy invaded and conquered England to become king in 1066. The Anglo-Saxon aristocracy was dispossessed and their land taken over by new Norman-French proprietors. French thereafter became the state language and remained so until the 15th century.

English, after a considerable struggle for survival and much altered by French influence, did not re-emerge as the court language until 1413. It was later reinforced by a long process of conquest or cultural domination; firstly of the neighbouring Celtic countries and then of a far-flung empire.

The empire has now gone, apart from the Celtic lands and a few minor overseas dependencies. Most of Ireland became independent in 1922. The gathering momentum for home rule has not yet succeeded in Wales and Scotland. When it does, as it will, much resentment will disappear and England's 'green and pleasant land' will be better placed to live in fruitful harmony with her neighbouring and equal nations.

The three lions in the English arms can be traced back to 1195 in the reign of Richard I. The crisp and dramatic red cross of St. George on a white field, which distinguishes the English flag, can be dated back to at least 1277. The St. George cross forms a component of the well known British Union Flag (or Jack).

IRELAND

The Gaelic sagas and myths deal with the origins of the Irish, and the ultimate triumph, in the 4th century, of the Gaels. Their rich culture and pagan mysticism was absorbed, rather than replaced, by the adoption of Christianity in the 5th century.

During Ireland's ensuing Golden Age her learning, craftsmanship and Christian devotion was a beacon to a crumbling Europe. The richness of this culture owed much to contact with Iberia, North Africa and the eastern Coptic tradition.

From the 8th century onwards Irish culture was threatened firstly by the Vikings and then increasingly from the 12th century by the English who exploited the country's resources while dispossessing the native Irish. The worst blow of all was the famine of 1845/8 through which a million died of starvation.

Not until 1919, after several years of violent struggle, was a new, mainly Catholic, 'Irish Free State' recognised. It did not, however, encompass all Ireland. Six northern counties, a majority of whose population were Protestants descended from English and Scottish settlers, elected to remain within Britain. This became the province of Northern Ireland.

The rival demands of the Protestant and Catholic communities in Northern Ireland for union respectively with Britain or Ireland will require a real effort of mutual understanding to reconcile.

The Irish (Gaelic) language suffered chronic decline in the 19th and 20th centuries. Despite encouragement, it languished until the 1980s when a revival occurred on both sides of the border.

The arms date from the 15th century, the flag from the 19th.

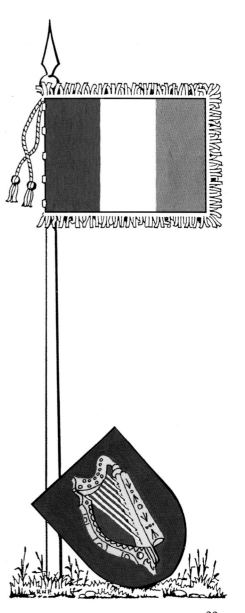

WALES

The people of this mountainous, ruggedly beautiful principality are the true inheritors of Celtic British culture. The Welsh language is essentially that spoken throughout most of Great Britain, and indeed much of Europe, in pre-Roman times.

Although Wales was conquered by King Edward I of England as early as 1284 and incorporated with England in 1536, the Welsh, of all the Celtic peoples, have been the most successful in retaining their linguistic and cultural identity against centuries of Anglicisation.

A major threat to Welsh throughout the 19th and 20th centuries has been the heavy emigration of Welsh speakers, coupled with the more damaging, in-migration of English settlers. In 100 years the proportion of the population which speaks Welsh has declined from around half to under 20%, or about 500,000 in total.

Against this trend, the second half of the 20th century has seen a remarkable revival in Welsh. Activists fostered the creation of official (and unofficial) support structures for effective language development. Major components have been the development of a network of Welsh-medium schools and more recently the creation of a Welsh-language television channel.

Much of Welsh administration is carried out by the Welsh Office, based in Cardiff, but there are no legislative or fiscal powers. A movement for political self-government, active for many years, has not yet been successful in its primary aim.

The venerable red dragon was the badge of Cadwallader, Prince of Gwynedd; white and green were the livery colours of Llewellyn, Prince of Wales. The arms and flag were officially adopted in 1959.

D > A or I

SCOTLAND

The original Scots were Gaelic-speaking people from northern Ireland. They settled first in the west of Scotland in the 5th century and then expanded north and east. In 843, Kenneth MacAlpine, King of Scots also became King of the Picts; the Kingdom of Alba was thus formed. By 1034 the Celtic Scots ruled almost all of what is present-day Scotland.

Long coveted by England, Scotland secured independence in 1314 by King Robert the Bruce's victory at the Battle of Bannockburn. In 1603, James VI, King of Scots succeeded to the English throne when Queen Elizabeth of England died. The two countries remained separate kingdoms, however, but under one monarch.

Independence came to an end in 1707 when, against the popular wish, the Scottish Parliament assented to Union with England. Thus Scotland lost its legislature but retains a separate administration, education system and Church. A majority of Scots now seeks reinstatement of the Scots Parliament.

Gaelic was the language of nearly all Scotland in the 13th century but has been subject to severe decline due to centuries of suppression. The 1980s have however seen a remarkable and vigorous revival in Gaelic.

With the retreat of Gaelic in the 14th century, Lallans, or Broad Scots (closely related to English) became the language of most Scots. With the loss of official status, this language too, although still widely understood, has suffered through the compulsory use of English in education and administration.

The arms of Scotland, with the distinctive double tressor, are very ancient, as is the Saltaire flag of St. Andrew.

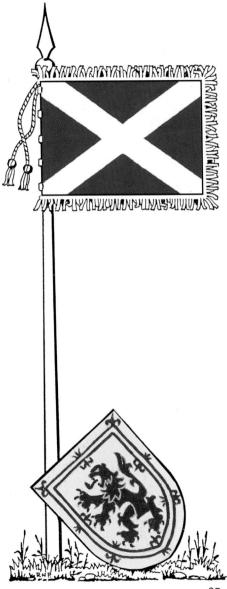

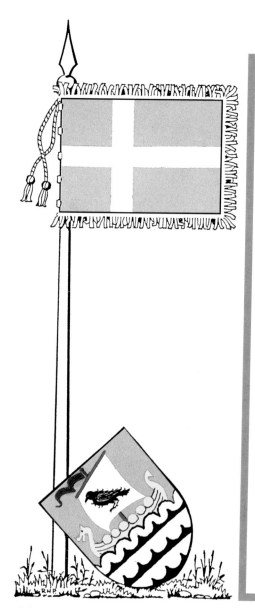

SHETLAND

Around AD 800, Shetland, an archipelago lying roughly mid-way between western Norway and the Faroe Islands, was colonised by Norsemen.

In 1469, by which time Shetland was a Danish possession, King Christian I, unable to pay the dowry for the wedding of his daughter Margaret to James III, King of Scots, pawned Shetland, together with the neighbouring islands of Orkney.

Shetland and Orkney were thus 'temporarily' transferred to the Scottish crown. Although language customs and laws were to be protected the islands became increasingly integrated with Scotland and in due course the United Kingdom. The old Norn language survived until the late 18th century and remains an influence today on the Shetland dialect of Scots.

In modern times the idea of home rule for Shetland emerged in 1962 after a local delegation witnessed at first hand the vigour of the autonomous Faroe Islands. In the mid 1970s concern about local government reorganisation and the threats and opportunities stemming from the discovery of North Sea oil fuelled this sentiment.

A political force known as the Shetland Movement emerged out of this process; it seeks to maximise local autonomy and control to protect local values and interests. The movement has a parallel, if less vociferous, counterpart in Orkney.

The arms are those of the Shetland Islands Council. The flag, a Scandinavian cross, designed in the 1960s by Shetland students, has become widely adopted in the islands in the face of official disapproval by Scotland's Lord Lyon King of Arms.

D > A

CORNWALL

The expansion westwards of the Saxons and the establishment of their kingdom of Wessex in the late 6th century, cut off the British Celts of the south west from their Celtic kin in Wales, Cumbria and Strathclyde. By the 8th century Celtic Dumnonia (Devon) crumbled, leaving Cornwall to stand alone.

Cornwall tenaciously retained its distinct Celtic language and customs, albeit under ever-increasing erosive pressure from, in turn, the Saxons, Normans and English. By the 18th century the language succumbed as a community language, although individuals who could speak some Cornish survived into the 19th century.

The 20th century has, however, seen a rebirth of Cornish national identity and a most remarkable resurrection of the old Celtic language. This stems from the efforts of a small group of scholars and enthusiasts. Several hundred Cornish people again use 'Kernewek'. These include a growing number of children for whom it is their mother tongue — for the first time in two centuries.

Cornwall is a member of the Celtic League, an association of activists representing the six Celtic countries of Scotland, Ireland, Wales, the Isle of Man and Brittany, as well as Cornwall itself.

The arms are those of the Duchy of Cornwall. The flag bears the cross of St. Piran, patron saint of Cornwall. It is seen everywhere in the Duchy, particularly on 5th March — St. Piran's Day.

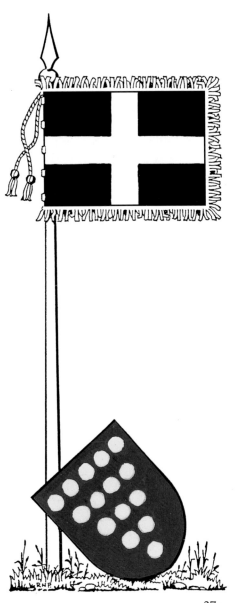

ISLE OF MAN

Located in the Irish Sea, mid-way between Great Britain and Ireland, this delightful island is said to have derived its name, 'Ellan Vannin' in Manx Gaelic, from the magical Celtic sea god Manainn MacLir who could summon at will a mantle of sea mist to make the island invisible to enemies.

Vikings first settled among the Celtic population in the 9th century and introduced a legislature, said to be the world's oldest, at Tynwald (*Ting vollr*, meaning assembly field in Norse).

The island was subsequently associated with the Hebrides, as part of the Lordship of the Isles which reached its zenith under Godred Crovan (King Orry). Between 1266 and 1405 the Isle of Man fell under first Scottish and then English dominance. After this its status as an independent lordship was re-established.

Today the Isle of Man is an independent micro state under the British crown. It has its own government, stamps, coins and tax regime. The Manx Gaelic language, very closely related to Irish and Scots Gaelic, was universally spoken in former times but declined throughout the 19th and 20th centuries. The last native speaker died in the 1970s. In recent decades there has been a revival in Manx language, music, dance, and culture.

The three legs of Man which appear on the arms and flag of the Isle of Man is a very old motif which was adopted by the Kings of Man in the 13th century.

JERSEY

Largest and southernmost of the Channel Islands, the Bailiwick of Jersey lies just 12 miles (19 km) from the Cotentin Peninsula of Normandy. The capital is St. Helier.

In 1204 Jersey separated from Normandy although it retained Norman law, customs and language. Administration was carried out for the King of England by a warden in the first instance, then subsequently by a captain, a governor, and from 1854, a lieutenant governor.

From 1617, justice and civil rights became matters for the bailiff through the Royal Court, as is also the case in Guernsey. Legislative powers were separated in 1771 and placed with the States of Jersey, now an elected body presided over by the bailiff, a Royal appointment.

The inhabitants are mainly of Norman, and to some extent Breton, descent and Norman French is Jersey's official language; indeed it is still used in the Royal Court. Considerable English immigration since 1830 has, however, caused the Norman language to decline greatly, and English is now predominant.

Jersey, like Guernsey, is a self-governing British Crown possession and neither a member of the United Kingdom nor the European Community. Tourism and its status as a tax haven sustain its economy.

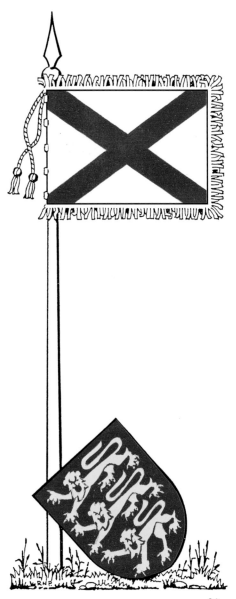

The arms of Jersey are almost identical to those of England, whose kings and queens have ruled Jersey since 1066. The flag dates from the mid 19th century.

I

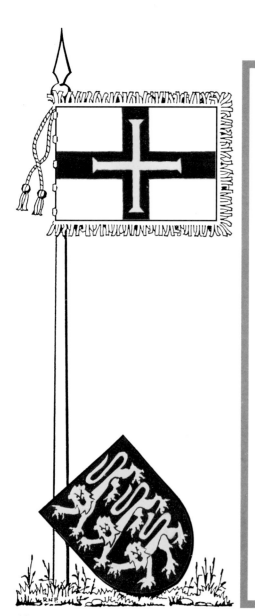

GUERNSEY

A separate Channel Islands jurisdiction from nearby Jersey, the Bailiwick of Guernsey has, like its neighbour, through historical chance, been left to run its own affairs for over 700 years.

Originally part of the Duchy of Normandy, the Channel Islands became linked to the English crown with the conquest of England by William, Duke of Normandy. When England lost her French possessions the islanders chose to remain with England and in return were given rights and privileges that have formed the basis of their independence ever since.

The islands are part of the British Isles but not of the United Kingdom, being self-governing in terms of laws and taxes and with a special relationship to the EC.

In addition to the main island of Guernsey, the Bailiwick comprises the smaller inhabited islands of Alderney, Sark, Herm, Jethou, Brecqhou and Lihou. Although they come under Guernsey's overall administration, Alderney and Sark have their own parliaments, flags and arms.

Traditionally Norman French in speech, English is the dominant language today.

The arms echo those of England but with the addition of a sprig of gold leaves. The flag again echoes that of England but, in the 1980s, a gold cross from the Bayeux tapestry was added for 'difference'.

The Low Countries
BENELUX

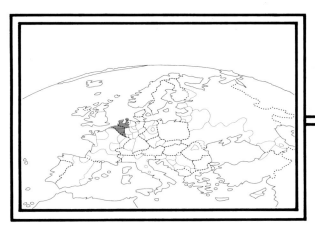

18 Netherlands 19 Friesland
20 Flanders 21 Wallonia
22 Luxemburg

The western extremity of the north European plain yields to the North Sea in the deltas of the great rivers Scheldt, Maas and Rhine amongst low heaths, sandy islands and dunes. By the 9th century Germanic Franks, Friesians and Saxons had settled all but the southernmost parts of these Low Countries, establishing a linguistic frontier between Germanic and Romance languages. This frontier remains essentially unchanged today.

For several centuries the Low Countries were pawns in the changing allegiances of local lords and the neighbouring powers. Unity eventually came when the Low Countries came under the control of the immensely powerful Burgundians. In the 15th century Flanders in particular flowered as a centre of commerce, art and urban development. In 1477 the Duchess Mary of Burgundy married Maximilian of Austria. The Low Countries thereafter became a Habsburg and in due course a Spanish appendage. With the Reformation and the adoption of Protestant ideas, particularly in the northern provinces, a violent and protracted revolt against Catholic Spanish rule brought eventual independence to the seven 'United Provinces' which by 1648 became the independent state of The Netherlands. The southern provinces remained Habsburg possessions until the French Revolution. A short period of French occupation was followed in 1814 by reunion with The Netherlands. A revolt in 1830 restored partition by creating a new independent Belgian kingdom. The Grand Duchy of Luxemburg was recognised as an independent state in 1867.

The modern and progressive constitutional monarchies of Belgium, The Netherlands and Luxemburg formed the 'Benelux' customs union in 1948 and were founder members of the European Economic Community (EEC), now known as the European Community (EC).

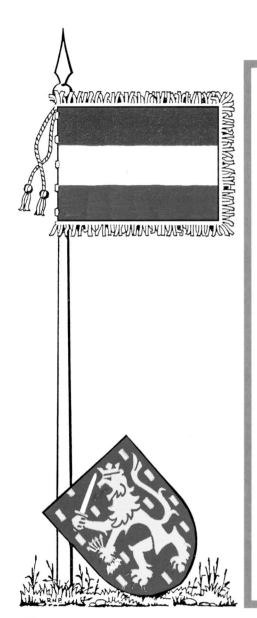

THE NETHERLANDS

The struggle to control the rivers and win land from the sea made The Netherlands. The struggle for religious and commercial freedom from the Spanish yoke brought independence.

In 1579 the seven mainly Protestant provinces north of the Rhine amalgamated under the Union of Utrecht, thereby creating a new Dutch nation state. By the 17th century the combined talents of merchants, artists, scientists and craftsmen created a high level of prosperity.

This Golden Age was sustained by the Province of Holland's pivotal position in European trade and the huge profits accruing from the monopoly of the Dutch East Indies Company based in Amsterdam. By the 18th century the glory had faded; by the end of that century the country was overrun by Napoleon's armies.

Independence was re-established in 1813 when the exiled William, Prince of Orange, was proclaimed the country's first king. Since that time The Netherlands has developed into a prosperous welfare state with a strong commitment to building the new Europe.

The lion of Orange-Nassau on a blue field strewn with billets (originally blocks of wood) is the main charge on the arms of The Netherlands. The sword and seven arrows (representing the original provinces) were symbols of the United Provinces. The flag was adopted in 1579 and was originally orange, white and blue, the livery colours of the House of Orange. Orange was replaced by red around 1630 to enhance recognition at sea.

I

FRIESLAND

The Frisians have lived along the coast of the North Sea for more than 2500 years. The Frisian language, distinct from Dutch and German, is related to Scots and Northern English. It is spoken by about 600,000 people today mainly in the Dutch province of Friesland but also in North Friesland (coastal areas and islands of the German *Land* of Schleswig-Holstein).

In East Friesland (part of the German *Land*, Lower Saxony) the Frisian language became extinct in the 19th century. Nevertheless the ethnic bond remains strong and the inhabitants still think of themselves as Frisians and participate in the Frisian Council formed in 1956.

Friesland had no feudal system in the Middle Ages, which encouraged the independence of Frisian farmers and traders. Their motto was 'free and Frisian'. The political independence of the West Frisians succumbed in 1798 with incorporation into the Dutch state. As early as 1525, however, the Frisian language ceased to be used officially and continued only as a vernacular.

A 'Frisian Movement' was created early in the 19th century to promote Frisian interests and in particular the language. Substantial progress has been made in rehabilitating Frisian. Its use is now permitted in court and since 1980 Frisian has been a compulsory subject in elementary school. Much remains to be done. A Frisian National Party was founded in the 1960s to press for greater autonomy for the Frisian people.

The Frisian arms date back to the Middle Ages but were officially confirmed only as recently as 1958. According to legend, the seven red water-lily leaves (not hearts) on the flag symbolise the seven medieval regions of Friesland. The flag in its present form dates from 1897.

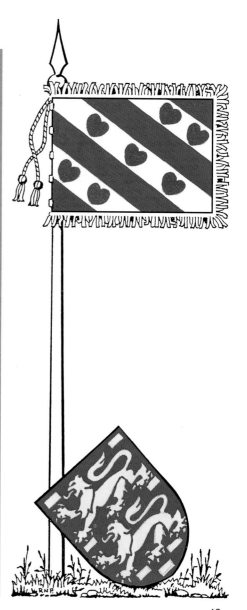

FLANDERS

The present day state of Belgium is divided by the long-standing linguistic border which separates the Dutch-speaking Flemings from the French-speaking Walloons. The dividing line actually extends westwards into the French state to meet the North Sea coast at Gravelines, just east of Calais.

During the 19th and first half of the 20th centuries, French was the ascendent and majority language in terms of administration, commerce and culture. In the second half of the 20th century, the balance of power and numbers has shifted to Flemish.

Once parity had been achieved, the rival ambitions of each linguistic group increasingly disrupted Belgian politics, to the extent that more and more power has been devolved to the separate linguistic regions. Flemish Nationalists see this as a stepping stone towards an independent Flanders. Brussels, the Belgian (and European) capital, while located in the Flemish zone, has a special bilingual status.

In the Westhoek-Dunkirk area of France some 200,000 people speak Flemish-Dutch, in spite of a long period of linguistic oppression by the French authorities.

The black lion rampant, with red claws on a yellow field, which forms the arms and flag of Flanders, is of great antiquity, dating from the beginnings of heraldry in the 12th century.

WALLONIA

The original Belgians were Celts who fought for seven years against the might of the Roman legions. Julius Caesar said of them 'Of all the Gallic people, the Belgians were the most courageous'. Despite their courage they had in the end to submit to the inevitable Romanising process. The Walloons of today, who occupy the southern portion of modern Belgium and parts of northern France, are their descendants.

Belgian Wallonia has been badly hit by economic decline during the second half of the 20th century. The population is just over 3 million. All speak French but some 450,000 can also speak the Walloon language as such. There are also small German-speaking communities of long standing located on the Belgian side of the German border.

The Walloon language, closely related to French, has been described as a Romance language with a Celtic substratum and Germanic influences. It has a substantial literature but no official status, although since 1983 teaching of the language in schools has been permitted and there is a small amount of broadcasting.

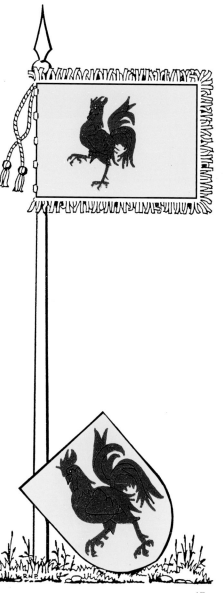

The red Gallic cock on a yellow field, featured on both the arms and flag of Wallonia, dates from 1913.

A > I

LUXEMBURG

When the Austrian (formerly Spanish) Netherlands passed to the United Netherlands in 1815, Luxemburg was attached to the new Kingdom and declared a Grand Duchy. With the breakaway of Belgium, Luxemburg, reduced in size, remained for a time a Dutch possession. In 1866, after the war between Austria and Germany had caused the demise of the German Confederation, of which Luxemburg had been part, the Grand Duchy became an independent micro state.

The national language of Luxemburg is a variety of German Moselle Frankish commonly known as *Lëtze-buergesh*. This Frankish language is also spoken in the Luxembourg province of Belgium, the territory detached from Luxemburg proper in 1830, but is there now completely supplanted by French in the schools and administration.

Today Luxemburg is a modern, prosperous democracy and home for several European institutions. Although virtually all the Grand Duchy's citizens speak *Lëtzebuergesh*, French and German are also used extensively such that multilingualism is almost universal.

The arms of the House of Luxemburg date from the 13th century. The flag was originally identical to that of The Netherlands but in due course the blue portion was made a lighter shade. As it is easily confused with the Dutch flag many Luxemburgers fly an unofficial flag charged with the arms or use the merchant flag which is the banner of the arms.

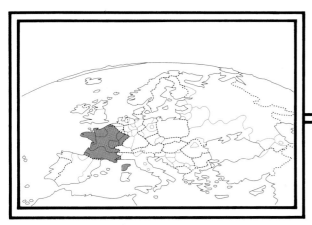

Old Gaul
THE FRENCH LANDS

23 France 24 Brittany
25 Normandy 26 Alsace
27 Lorraine 28 Burgundy
29 Occitania 30 Monaco
31 Andorra 32 Corsica

Celtic Gaul, approximating geographically with modern France, fell by stages to the might of Rome. By the end of the 2nd century BC, Gallia Narbonensis in the south had become a 'Provincia Romana', from which comes the name Provence, and to this day it remains the most 'Latin' part of France.

The rest of Gaul was brought into the Empire within the next century: 400 years of Romanisation ensued. Although most Gauls, in time, adopted the Latin tongue, a Celtic flavour remained to influence the development of the French language.

After the sack of Rome in AD 410, 'civilised' Europe was open to massive in-migration of 'barbarian' Germanic tribes such as Goths, Vandals, Franks and Burgundians. From among these the Franks emerged to conquer much of Gaul. Their king, Clovis, was baptised a Christian in AD 496.

The Frankish kingdom and the Church grew in power and eventually provided the base from which Charlemagne was able to establish a vast European empire with its capital in Aachen. On Christmas Day, 800, the Pope crowned Charlemagne as emperor.

The Carolingian Empire did not last. In 843 it was divided among Charlemagne's grandsons: Louis, who took Germany; Lothair, who took the central strip from the Low Countries, through Burgundy to Italy; and Charles, who inherited the land of the western Franks, which in due course came to be known as France.

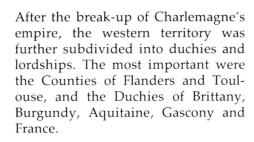

FRANCE

After the break-up of Charlemagne's empire, the western territory was further subdivided into duchies and lordships. The most important were the Counties of Flanders and Toulouse, and the Duchies of Brittany, Burgundy, Aquitaine, Gascony and France.

Of these, the (then small) Duchy of France became pre-eminent and evolved into Europe's first kingdom when Hugh Capet seized the crown in 987. The Capetian line ruled France continuously thereafter until deposed by the 1789 French Revolution.

In the 18th century French power and prestige were supreme. French had become the language of diplomacy throughout Europe and has subsequently become a major world language.

As the central authority of Paris grew so were its values imposed. For example the 1539 Edict of Villers-Cotterets made French the only official language within the king's jurisdiction. This was much to the detriment of other languages, such as the 'langue d'oc' spoken over a wide area in the south.

The French state of today continues to embrace a rich and precious diversity of indigenous linguistic minorities, despite centuries of suppression by the centralising policies of Paris. These peoples are: Catalans, Corsicans, Occitans, Germans, Dutch, Bretons and Basques. Each seeks, and deserves, greater scope for self-determination.

The beautiful fleur-de-lis arms of France date back, in one form or other, to the 12th century. Although no longer the state emblem they are still widely regarded as the real symbol of France. The famous tricolour flag dates from the French Revolution of 1789.

BRITTANY

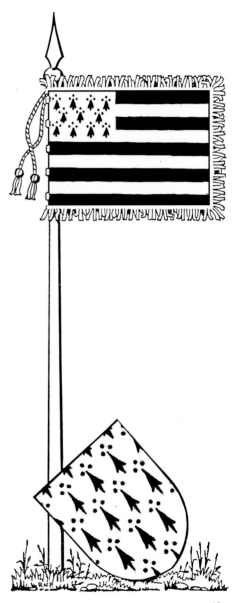

The 5th century saw a large migration by sea of Celtic people from Britain and Ireland to the western part of the Armorican peninsula which was to become Britanny.

Long coveted by the French kings, Brittany kept its independence for many centuries as a powerful duchy. In 1532, however, she came under the authority of the French crown. Provincial autonomy survived until the French Revolution when Brittany was wholly incorporated within the French state.

During much of the 20th century the Breton people have had to suffer the double burden of economic decline and linguistic oppression by the French authorities. The Breton language (a Celtic language akin to Welsh), still spoken by an estimated 600,000 people, has had no place in education or official life.

Since the 1960s, however, there has been a growing sense of Breton national identity and a revival of interest in the rich heritage of Breton music, culture and language. Of particular importance has been the establishment of Breton language pre-school playgroups and schools run by the voluntary Diwan organisation, albeit with official obstruction.

An unfortunate irritation to national feeling has been that the traditionally Breton Nantes area has not been included in the new administrative region of Brittany.

The distinctive 13th century black and white ermine arms are those of the Duchy of Brittany. The flag is extensively and enthusiastically flown by Bretons as a statement of nationality. The stripes represent the traditional divisions of independent Brittany.

D > A or I

NORMANDY

The Normans were originally pagan Scandinavian Viking seafarers who made plundering raids on the European coast in the 8th and 9th centuries.

By about 900 they had established a permanent settlement in the lower Seine valley. In 911 the Frankish king, Charles III (the Simple) ceded land to Rollo, the Viking leader. In time this holding extended to become the powerful Duchy of Normandy.

The Normans converted to Christianity and adopted the French language. They continued to display a capacity for courageous fighting, cunning and enterprising manipulation of power. Their creation of the feudal system was an enduring legacy.

The Normans undertook several major campaigns in Sicily and, importantly, the invasion and conquest of England by William (the Bastard) Duke of Normandy in 1066. He thereafter became King of England, with which country Normandy was linked until 1450. From that time Normandy came under permanent French control, being created a province in 1468. In 1791 the French revolutionary government abolished the province and created five departments in its place.

Today Normandy is divided into two separate planning regions, but Norman identity remains sufficiently strong that a 'United Normandy' movement is active in seeking more autonomy for a single Norman province. The Norman patois which contains English and Norse words is unfortunately in decline.

The arms are closely related to those of England. The flag, a Scandinavian cross based on the livery colours of the arms, is used by the 'Unite' activists.

ALSACE

The Duchy of Alsace was founded in the 5th century. From the 10th to the 17th century, it formed part of the Holy Roman Empire although divided into numerous lordships and municipalities inhabited by German speakers.

French influence became dominant after the Peace of Westphalia (1648) placed Alsace under the informal protection of France. Until the end of the 18th century Alsace retained a considerable degree of autonomy under the French crown, but with the French Revolution full incorporation within France was accomplished.

Because of the large German-speaking population, Alsace, together with part of Lorraine, was claimed by Germany and, after the French defeat in the Franco-German War, these territories were incorporated into the German Empire in 1871.

In 1919 Alsace/Lorraine returned to France and in the 1920s a home rule movement emerged seeking autonomy within the French Republic. During the Second World War Alsace/Lorraine was reannexed to Germany and again returned to France in 1945.

Alsace now forms a 'planning region' of France, capital Strasbourg, but there is as yet little real autonomy. Although French is the official language the majority of the population speak an Alemanic dialect of German which has slowly been regaining recognition and support through the insistence of cultural associations and municipalities.

The arms are medieval and the flag is that used by the Alsatian autonomy movement.

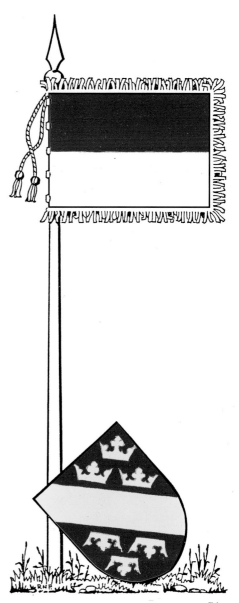

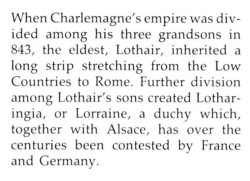

LORRAINE

When Charlemagne's empire was divided among his three grandsons in 843, the eldest, Lothair, inherited a long strip stretching from the Low Countries to Rome. Further division among Lothair's sons created Lotharingia, or Lorraine, a duchy which, together with Alsace, has over the centuries been contested by France and Germany.

Although Lorraine has been incorporated within the French state since 1945, the speech of the people is traditionally a German Frankish dialect. It is still widely spoken but its use has been discouraged by the French authorities. Since the 1970s, however, pressure for protection and recognition has been growing in effectiveness.

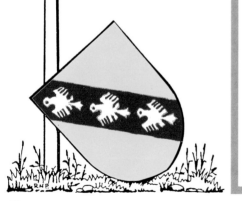

The earliest record of the arms of Lorraine dates from 1207. They consist of a gold field with a red bend charged with three silver alerions (heraldic eagles without beak or claws), traditionally attributed to the miraculous piercing, by Godfrey de Bouillon, of three birds with a single arrow! The flag echoes that of neighbouring Alsace.

D > A

BURGUNDY

The presence of the Germanic Burgundians in the Rhône-Saône valleys dates back to the 5th century. By tradition Burgundy proper covers the Duchy of Burgundy (capital Dijon), long part of France, and the County of Burgundy, later known as Franche-Comté (capital Besançon), long outwith France and part of the Holy Roman Empire.

By the 15th century the Dukes of Burgundy ruled a vast rich area which in addition to the Burgundian lands as such, included much of what is now Belgium, The Netherlands, Alsace and Lorraine. These dukes were more powerful than most kings of the period.

After many dynastic alignments, such as with Spain and Austria, and after eventual dismemberment, Burgundy was absorbed into the French state. Today the planning regions of Burgundy and Franche-Comté each have a very limited and separate measure of devolved administration for the first time since the French Revolution.

The old Germanic tongue of the Burgundians is long extinct, French being the language in use today.

The arms (Burgundy Ancient) date from the 13th century. In 1364 Philip the Bold quartered these arms with those of Touraine (Burgundy Modern), a combination which still symbolises the Region of Burgundy. The beautiful old flag of Burgundy — a red St. Andrew's Saltaire raguly — was the emblem of the Knights of the Golden Fleece, one of Europe's most illustrious orders of chivalry. It is little known by modern Burgundians but in its day, because of dynastic links, this flag has also flown over Spain and its former dominions, including Belgium and Latin America. It deserves a comeback in the land of its birth.

OCCITANIA

The large territory of the 'Pays d'Oc' covers most of the south of France: thirty-one departments, or about one-third of the whole state, the western valleys of the Italian Alps and the Val d'Aran within the Spanish state. Altogether it embraces some twelve million people.

The language, with its several dialect forms, is more Latin in character than French. It has a dazzling and prestigious past which influenced all Medieval Europe through its troubadours. The different states which made up the Occitan territory were, however, never truly unified and fell one by one to France.

During the 20th century the language has been under serious threat through pressure of French, the only language permitted in public use. Today only about 10% speak Occitan.

The Institute of Occitan Studies was formed in 1945 to take on the daunting task of defending and developing the Occitan language and culture. A major achievement has been the fostering of a revival of contemporary Occitan publishing. A limited amount of mainly voluntary Occitan teaching is also now available.

An ongoing feature of the Occitan revival is a conflict between 'pan Occitanism' and a tendency for regionalisation. The strength of the adjacent and closely related Catalan renaissance has on the other hand boosted Occitan confidence.

The arms are those of the Counts of Tolosa (Toulouse), most influential of the medieval Occitan dynasties. The flag is a banner of the arms, although the yellow flag with four vertical stripes is also used.

D > A

MONACO

This sovereign principality and micro state is located on the Mediterranean coast of southern France close to the Italian border. It extends to only 1.9 sq km and has come under the ownership of the Grimaldi family almost continuously since 1297.

After interruption caused by the French Revolution, Monaco's sovereign independence was restored in 1861 under a treaty with France.

Monaco is in a customs union with France (and therefore the EC) but maintains its own liberal tax regime. Like other micro states it issues its own stamps. The main industry is tourism, encouraged by the famous casino of Monte Carlo. Popular attention was focused upon the principality in 1956 when Prince Rainier III married the American actress Grace Kelly.

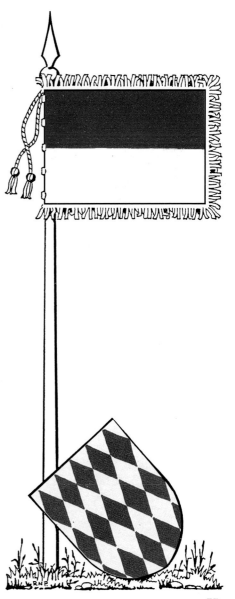

The princely arms consist of fifteen red diamonds on a white field. The bi-colour flag reflects the colours of the arms.

ANDORRA

This ancient micro state, located in a once remote valley in the Pyrenees, has borders with both France and Spain.

Its independent status dates back to 1278 when the Bishop of Urgel and the Count of Foix jointly arranged to be responsible for the sovereignty of the principality. The arrangement persists to this day, save that the French President carries out the role of the Count of Foix in nominating a proportion of Andorra's judicial officers.

The principality, whose capital is Andorra la Vella, has the normal trappings of statehood, including the issue of stamps. It has, however, no currency of its own; both French francs and Spanish pesetas are used. The economy today is based mainly on duty free retail sales and winter ski tourism. As Europe's premier tax haven Andorra has a sizeable expatriate community.

The state language is Catalan.

The quarterings of Andorra's arms represent the mitre and crosier of the Bishop of Urgel; the three vertical stripes of the Count of Foix; the two cows of his successor, the Count of Bearn; and the four red vertical stripes of Catalonia. The flag dates from 1866 and for official use is charged with the arms. A variation uses horizontal stripes with or without a count's coronet in the centre.

CORSICA

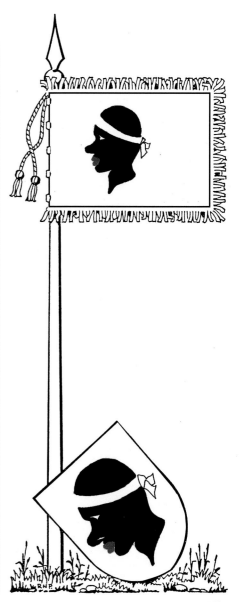

This large mountainous Mediterranean island is known as the 'Scented Isle' because of the fragrance of the flowers of the *maquis*, or undergrowth, which carries far out to sea. It remains substantially covered by wild luxuriant vegetation.

Over the last two millennia, Corsica has been at different times under the control of Romans, Vandals, Byzantines, Lombards, Franks, the Pope and Pisa. In the mid 15th century it came under Genoan administration.

The island enjoyed self-government for a brief period in the 18th century but it was not to last. In 1769 it was made a province of France. The same year, Corsica's most famous son, Napoleon, was born.

Since that time the French language has been promoted by the authorities. This policy was reinforced in the 1960s by a large influx of French-speaking, former Algerian, settlers. In spite of this, and the debilitating effect of heavy emigration, some 200,000 still speak Corsican, a language akin to Tuscan.

The language and culture is nonetheless under serious threat. A vociferous nationalist movement has emerged which seeks political and cultural self-determination for the Corsicans. Among nationalist demands, top priority is given to the promotion of the language in education, the media and in public life.

The rather macabre arms and flag of Corsica, which are widely used, representing a severed Moor's head, make reference to the early struggle by the Corsicans against the Muslims.

D > A or I

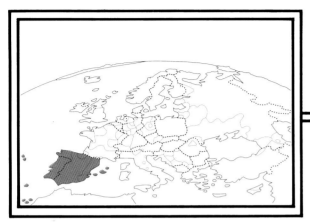

The Iberian Peninsula
SPAIN AND PORTUGAL

33 Castille 34 Catalonia
35 Euskadi 36 Galicia
37 Canary Islands 38 Portugal
39 Madeira 40 Azores
41 Gibraltar

This rectangular land mass, bounded by the sea and the formidable mountain barrier of the Pyrenees, defines the south-western extremity of continental Europe. Many ethnic groups have occupied the peninsula and left their mark, among them the Basques whose mysterious origin pre-dates the Indo-European immigrations from the east some 3000 years ago. Archaeological evidence suggests that the Basques are the last survivors of western Europe's aboriginal population.

Subsequent Indo-European arrivals include Celts, Romans, Visigoths and Vandals who migrated from the north. In the 8th century AD, with the explosive expansion of Islam, a great wave of Moors (Muslim Arabs and Berbers) invaded and established a level of civilised life unknown elsewhere in Western Europe. Within this Islamic society, Christians were tolerated, the arts flourished and technical advances were fostered. It was extinguished in the closing decade of the 15th century, although from the 11th century onwards the power struggle between Christian and Moor was to dominate political life. Only on the northern fringe had small Christian kingdoms survived. It was they who were to be the progenitors of the mighty, all-conquering Catholic kingdoms and empires of Spain and Portugal which, with the opening up of sea routes to Africa, the East and the Americas, were, for better or worse, to introduce European values to the world.

The story of rise and eventual decline echoes that of all empires. After a sterile period in the middle years of the 20th century, when both Portugal and Spain were ruled by Fascist dictators, a fresh and exciting wind of democracy has rekindled a new sense of purpose and zest for liberty.

CASTILLE

Out of the long struggle to reconquer Spain from the Moors, emerged Castille. Originally a mere county of Leon, it came to dominate the other Christian kingdoms, particularly after union with Aragon when the 'Catholic Kings', Fernando and Isabella, completed the reconquest with the capture of Granada in 1492.

In that same year Columbus discovered America for Spain, thereby opening up the New World to conversion, colonisation and exploitation. A vast Spanish Empire was created and extended through strategic marriage alliances to include the Low Countries, Austria and the Two Sicilies.

Immense wealth flowed from the Americas, and the Spain of the 'Golden' 16th century was undoubtedly the world's leading power. As a consequence Spanish is today the world's third most widely spoken language.

From the mid-17th century fortunes reversed. Losing first her European and then her American possessions, Spain was thrown back upon herself. The late 19th and early 20th centuries saw much social and political unrest, culminating in the Civil War (1936–39) and the Franco dictatorship.

With the death of Franco in 1975, Spain was transformed into a model democratic constitutional monarchy with one of the fastest growing economies in Europe. Varying degrees of self rule have been granted to 17 new regions with special powers of autonomy to Euskadi (the Basques), Catalonia and Galicia.

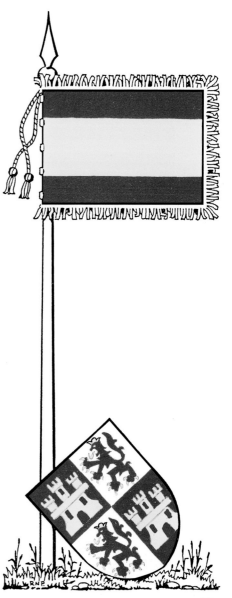

The arms of the united kingdoms of Leon and Castille date from 1230 and are the earliest known examples of quartering. The flag dates from a royal decree of 1785.

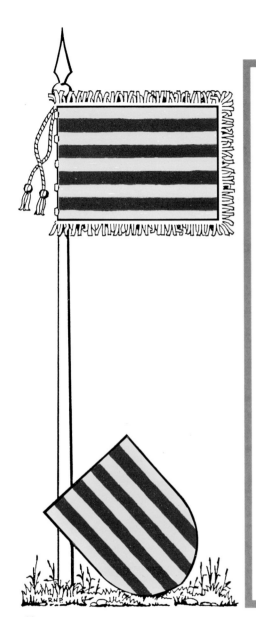

CATALONIA

From the 12th to the 14th century Catalonia, with Aragon, flourished in a Golden Age noted for maritime and commercial prowess. In 1359 the Catalan Generalitat was established as one of Europe's first parliamentary governments.

When Fernando V of Aragon married Isabella of Castille, most of Catalonia was incorporated into the emerging Spanish state. In the ensuing centuries, however, the Catalans never lost their desire for independence.

A Catalan Republic was created between 1931 and 1939 only to be crushed by Franco in the closing months of the Civil War. Thirty-six years of linguistic, cultural and political repression followed.

With the restoration of democracy, a new autonomous Catalan Generalitat was formed in 1977. Separate less far reaching autonomous arrangements were also created in the Catalan-speaking Balearic Islands and Valencia.

Of all Europe's 'minority' languages, Catalan (closely related to Occitan) is the strongest. It is more widely spoken than several national state languages. In Catalonia proper it is the language of regional and local government, commerce, the media and education, and has a large literary output.

The situation elsewhere is less satisfactory, particularly in the long-standing Catalan-speaking parts of south-eastern France where there is as yet virtually no official linguistic support.

The arms date from the 12th century when Catalonia united with Aragon. The flag is the banner of the arms.

3A & D > Im

EUSKADI/NAVARRA

The complex Euskara language, distinct from any other, is thought to be the most ancient in Europe. Although once more extensive, the Basque lands nowadays cover, in Spain, the three Basque Provinces proper, much of Navarra, and also part of south-west France. Traditionally the capital is Iruna (Pamplona).

Since the 9th century the kingdom of Navarra largely provided for the political governance of the Basques. In 1515 the larger southern part of Navarra was absorbed by Spain while the area north of the Pyrenees became part of France. The Basques nevertheless jealously defended their sense of independence.

The Spanish Civil War was a disaster for the Basques. Under the subsequent Franco regime, the ancient rights of autonomy were disregarded, the language and culture suppressed, and a policy of Hispanicisation pursued.

With the reinstatement of democracy in Spain autonomy was restored to the Basque Provinces in 1978, since when an intense revival of language and culture has been underway. Separately, Navarra has been given lesser powers of autonomy but with the option of eventual union with the Basque Provinces. The Basques in France as yet receive little recognition.

Although much progress has been made towards self-determination, many Basques nurture the vision of reunification of all the Basque lands, so re-creating the old concept of Navarra.

The Basques currently use quartered arms, but the old arms of Navarra, attributed to the carrying off by King Sancho of chains protecting the camp of Muhamad bin Yusuf in 1212, here presage a reunified land. The Basque flag originated in the 19th century.

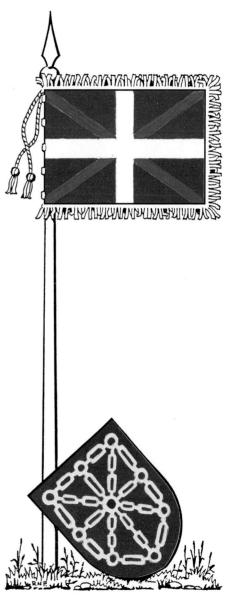

GALICIA

This land in the far north-west corner of Spain has, in appearance, a closer similarity to Ireland or Brittany than to the rest of Spain.

Its people, too, are said to be descended from a Celtic race and although the old Celtic tongue is long extinct, a powerful, spiritual, musical and poetic tradition certainly persists which may confirm these origins.

Although the demand for self-government in Galicia is more recent than in Euskadi and Catalonia, a strong Galician identity was encouraged through the work of influential 19th and 20th century artists, poets and writers such as Rosalia de Castro and Antonio Castelao. They raised the status of the Gallego tongue (akin to Portuguese) in the popular and official mind from what was regarded as a rustic dialect to a national language.

After years of repression under Franco, Gallego is now obligatory in all Galician schools, along with Castilian Spanish. Gallego is also the language of the Galician parliament and administration, and has full exposure on radio and television.

It is estimated that Gallego is spoken by approximately two thirds of the population and is understood by about 90%.

The 15th century arms, readopted by the new Galician Parliament in 1978, reflect the place of the Catholic Church in the development of Galicia, particularly as Santiago de Compostela, the capital, was in medieval times, one of the most important places of Christian pilgrimage. In the flag, which dates from the 19th century, white traditionally represents Galicia and the blue bend represents the sea.

CANARY ISLANDS

Called the 'Fortunate Islands' since ancient times, the Canaries lie off the African coast and were originally inhabited by aboriginal people called Guanches. Spanish conquest, island by island, began in 1402. This long, cruel and bloody process took almost a century to complete.

Columbus took on board his last provisions in the Canaries prior to his epic transatlantic crossing of 1492. From that time onwards the islands became a bridge between the Old World and the New. Over the centuries many Canarians settled in Latin America, with which there remains considerable contact. The lilting Canarian dialect of Spanish is in fact very similar to that of Cuba.

The Canaries were never regarded as a colony but were from the start integrated into Spain. In 1927 two provinces were created, for there had long been pressure for more autonomy. Further progress towards this was not, however, possible until the mid 1970s when the new climate of democracy and pluralism was grasped with enthusiasm.

Under the Statute of Autonomy of 1982, the Canary Islanders now have the opportunity to control their political and economic destiny through their own parliament and administration.

The arms adopted by the Canarian Parliament represent the seven main islands. The now official white, blue and yellow flag has been used unofficially in various forms as a symbol of autonomy for about 100 years.

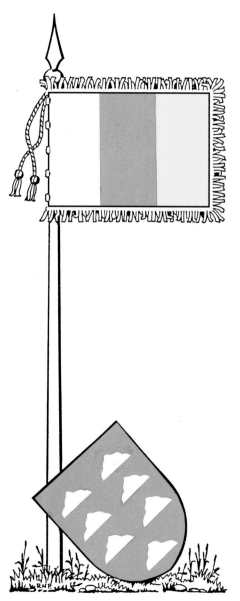

PORTUGAL

Founded around 1100, Portugal's boundaries have remained fixed since the 13th century. This tenacious nation has its roots in the period immediately following the expulsion of the Moors. Driven by a hatred of heresy and a deep suspicion of Spain, Portugal developed as a separate single nation.

Portugal's age of discovery, during which Portuguese sailors opened up the world to Europe, preceded Spain's overseas conquests. These pioneering voyages spawned vast colonial possessions such that Portuguese is now the world's fifth most widely spoken language.

From 1580, when Portugal lost both king and army in a Moroccan war, the country suffered centuries of adversity including absorption by Spain for sixty years, the loss of Brazil in 1822 and finally national bankruptcy in the early 20th century.

For half a century thereafter Portugal endured an isolationist dictatorship which rendered it Europe's poorest country by the 1960s. Following a coup in 1974, however, democracy was reinstated with a consequent renewed sense of purpose and freedom.

The five small blue shields arranged in a cross in the arms of Portugal originated in the 12th century. The border with seven castles was added in the 13th century. The old blue and white flag was discarded with the monarchy in 1910 and the present version was introduced by the republic. It is charged with the arms supported on an armillary sphere — an old nautical instrument alluding to the period of Portugal's maritime prowess.

MADEIRA

First explored by Genoese adventurers in the 14th century, the formerly uninhabited Atlantic island of Madeira and the neighbouring island of Porto Santo were colonised by the Portuguese, as part of their quest for trade and territory, in the 1420s. The islands' forests were burnt down to create cultivable land. It is said that the fires raged for seven years!

Madeira is believed to have been the location of the world's first sugar cane plantation. Today, this crop has been partially superseded by bananas, stock raising and wine production, including the famous 'Madeira' fortified wine. The congenial climate also attracts a considerable retirement and year-round tourist trade.

With the restoration of democracy in Portugal following the 1974 coup, Madeira was given the status of an autonomous region of Portugal. For the first time, it was given its own administration controlled by a democratically elected assembly, albeit so far with limited powers.

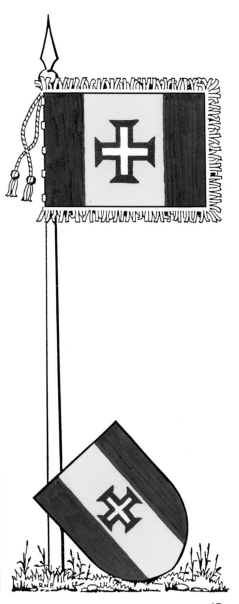

As there had been no traditional arms and flag for the region, the government, in 1978, adopted a new design featuring the cross of the 'Order of Christ', a characteristically Portuguese motif. The blue is for the sea, nobility, beauty and serenity; and the gold is for the climate, wealth, strength, faith, purity and constancy.

AZORES

This group of volcanic islands, located in the mid-Atlantic some 740 miles west of São Miguel in Portugal, was discovered around 1427 by Diogo de Senill, a Portuguese royal pilot. No traces of human habitation were found. Portuguese settlement began about 1432.

The main products today are fruit and wine although the islands were formerly a major whaling centre. The population of about 250,000 speak Portuguese.

Until modern times the Azores were regarded as an integral part of Portugal but the democratisation of Portugal in the 1970s brought the Azores a small measure of local power. Many Azorans, however, seek more substantial autonomy.

The arms of the Azores feature a goshawk surrounded by nine stars, representing the nine major islands. Their use had been prohibited prior to 1822, after which variants of the design were used on documents of the local authorities. The flag is of modern origin, echoes the colours on the flag of the old Portuguese monarchy and often carries the hawk and stars emblem.

GIBRALTAR

Captured from Spain by the British in 1704, 'the Rock' has been a British Crown Colony since the Treaty of Utrecht in 1713. This state of affairs has long been disputed by Spain which seeks its return.

The views of local people to both Britain and Spain are ambivalent, but as one of Britain's last colonies, whose strategic significance is now much less than formerly, it seems likely that in due course some form of accommodation may be reached between the two states.

The colony gained a measure of self-government in 1969 and local currency and stamps are now issued. It is possible that a political settlement may result in the emergence of Gibraltar as one of the growing number of European micro states but linked with Spain.

Although English is currently the official language, the Gibraltarians, who are of mixed origin, speak Yanito, a variant of Andalusian Spanish.

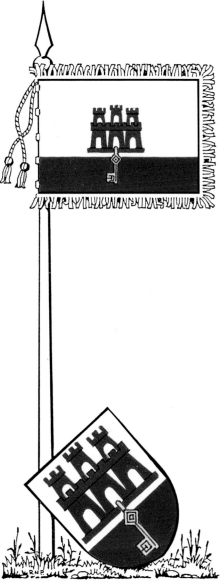

The castle and key on the arms of Gibraltar symbolise the strategic position of Gibraltar as key to the Mediterranean. The official flag of the colony is the Union Flag of Britain, but the unofficial National Flag illustrated, which is the banner of the arms, was introduced in 1966.

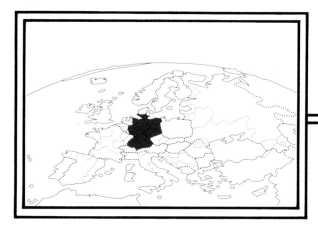

42 Schleswig Holstein 43 Hamburg
44 Bremen 45 Hanover
46 Brunswick Lüneburg
47 Oldenburg 48 Schaumberg-Lippe
49 Westphalia 50 Rhineland
51 Hesse 52 Palatinate
53 Saarland 54 Swabia
55 Bavaria 56 Berlin
57 Brandenburg 58 Mecklenburg
59 Pomerania 60 Thuringia
61 Saxony

The Fatherland
GERMANY

In the great pre-dark-age migrations, German tribes occupied their heartland between North Sea, western Baltic and the Alps. The Frankish empire of Charlemagne (771 to 814) completed the Christianising of the formerly heathen Germans and established an eastern frontier between German and Slav on the Elbe/Saale rivers. 'Marches' were created east of this line to protect the frontier, from which an eastwards colonisation into Slav territory commenced. With the division of the Carolingian Empire the eastern portion evolved into five great duchies. In 962 the Pope crowned Saxon King Otto the Great as emperor. This was the origin of what came to be known as the Holy Roman Empire of the German Nation. Emperors were elected by a college of princes who generally chose as weak a monarch as possible. Local principalities had almost complete independence. In time, as land was divided by inheritance, Germany became a mosaic of several hundred states.

The Holy Roman Empire was swept away in 1806, permitting Prussia, the strongest of the German states, eventually to bring the others into, firstly, a customs union and then in 1871 a Second Empire or Reich. This Second Reich fell in 1918 with defeat in the Great War. Hitler's even shorter lived '1000 year' Third Reich was extinguished in 1945 after nearly six years of world war.

Germany was then partitioned by the Allies: the easternmost part was absorbed into Poland and the USSR, the Soviet Zone became the German Democratic Republic (GDR, or (Communist) East Germany) and the remainder became the Federal Republic of Germany (West Germany). With the democratisation of Eastern Europe, and the GDR in particular, unification of the two Germanies into a single Fatherland followed as a natural consequence in 1990.

SCHLESWIG HOLSTEIN

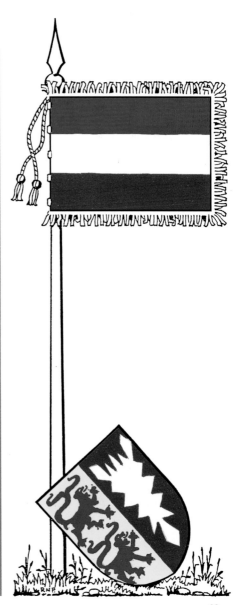

The new West Germany, created from the ruins of the Second World War, became a federal republic of nine new or reconstituted states plus West Berlin. Each state or *Land*, except West Berlin, gained a large measure of autonomous self-government.

Land Schleswig Holstein is the most northerly of these *Länder*. It occupies much of the territory at the base of the Jutland peninsula covered by the formerly separate duchies of Schleswig, to the north, and Holstein, to the south.

The strategic position as a link between Germany and Scandinavia and as a bridge between the Baltic and the North Sea, brought immense prosperity to the Hanseatic town of Lübeck. It was also the focus over the centuries of a struggle for control between German and Dane.

The conflict was renewed in the 1860s by the complex question of the Schleswig Holstein succession, in which the duchies were claimed by both Danes and Germans. They were seized by Prussia in the war of 1864. North Schleswig with its Danish population was returned to Denmark following a plebiscite in 1920.

The natural language of Schleswig Holstein is Low German, although today High German is used officially and is increasingly prevalent in everyday speech. A small Danish-speaking community, whose rights are protected, lives close to the border with Denmark. There are also communities of North Frisian speakers on the west coast and offshore islands.

The arms show, dexter the lions of Schleswig, and sinister the nettle leaf of Holstein, both ancient blazons. The flag, adopted 1957, is an amalgamation of the flags of the old duchies.

HAMBURG

Around 820 on a dry spur, at the confluence of the Alster and the Elbe, a Carolingian fortress called the Hammaburg was established. Below it, among the creeks, grew a settlement of sailors and merchants.

Lübeck chose Hamburg as its North Sea trans-shipment point on the overland trade route from the Baltic. Thereafter its importance as a member of the Hanseatic League grew. The *Hanse* was an association of independent northern towns which flourished on maritime trade in the 14th and 15th centuries.

Access to the North Sea enabled Hamburg to profit in later years from the development of ocean routes to America and Asia. Gradually it developed into a great cosmopolitan port and industrial city with the Elbe river system providing access to its hinterland.

Hamburg's independent status is recognised today as it constitutes a federal *Land* in its own right, under the title of Free and Hanseatic City of Hamburg.

The arms of Hamburg can be traced back to around 1100, red and white being Hanseatic colours. The traditional flag shown has appeared in various versions over the years and is based on the arms. The current official version shows the full coat of arms on a rectangular white panel on a red field.

Af

BREMEN

Located on a historic river crossing at the head of the Weser estuary, Bremen's origin is a bishop's church built in 788 to promote the conversion of the northern Germans to Christianity. Like Hamburg, Bremen evolved as a trading city state and port.

The increasing size of ships and the silting up of the river caused outports of Vegsack and Bremerhaven to be created, but with the dredging of the Weser in 1887, ocean ships could again berth in the city.

One year later Bremen joined the German Customs Union. This gave the port's trade a major boost to rank as Germany's second largest. Trade with North and South America has been particularly important.

Today Bremen, together with Bremerhaven, form the smallest *Land* of the Federal Republic as the Free Hanseatic City of Bremen.

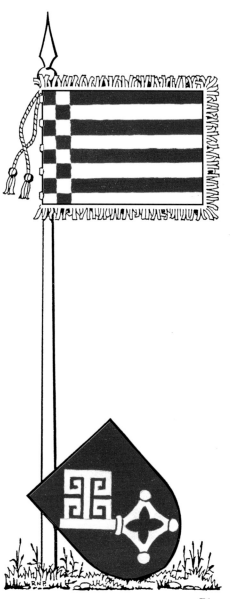

The silver key in the arms has been used as a heraldic charge by the old Hanseatic city since 1366 and represents the apostle St. Peter, patron saint of Bremen. The distinctive striped flag also dates from the Middle Ages. An official version today carries the arms in a white panel.

HANOVER

The Province of Hanover was long associated with the House of Guelph and the Dukes of Brunswick-Lüneburg. The town of Hanover developed as a flourishing medieval market place and from 1635 to 1866 was state capital.

Between 1714 and 1837 the Electors of Hanover were also Kings of Great Britain. The death of the British King William IV in 1837 separated the two thrones, because Victoria, as a woman, could not succeed to Hanover.

As part of the post-war restructuring of Germany, Hanover, along with Brunswick-Lüneburg, Oldenburg, and Schaumberg-Lippe, were amalgamated in 1945 to form the new federal *Land* of Lower Saxony (capital Hanover).

In many respects Lower Saxony constitutes a more logical unit of government than the former states which evolved through the vicissitudes of princely fortune. Nevertheless, the identities of the old states, with their sense of historical continuity, still hold an affection in the popular consciousness.

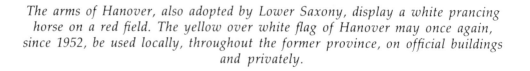

The arms of Hanover, also adopted by Lower Saxony, display a white prancing horse on a red field. The yellow over white flag of Hanover may once again, since 1952, be used locally, throughout the former province, on official buildings and privately.

Df [> Af]

BRUNSWICK-LÜNEBURG

The name Brunswick comes from a certain Bruno, original Lord of Brunswick. In the 12th century Henry the lion, Duke of Brunswick and Luneburg, married Matilda, eldest daughter of Henry II of England. This may be the origin of the two gold lions, or heraldic leopards, on the red shield of Brunswick.

This line became the House of Guelph, which was also closely linked with neighbouring Hanover. Brunswick (capital Brunswick) existed as an independent state within the German Reich until 1945, after which it merged with the new *Land* of Lower Saxony, within the German Federal Republic.

As elsewhere in Germany, High German is the official language. Many in Brunswick-Lüneburg, however, continue to use Low German in everyday speech, being the natural language of northern Germany and closely related to Dutch and Flemish. Sadly, Low German receives little official recognition or support, which, coupled with post-war in-migration of non-Low German speakers, has led to the decline of this historically important language.

The arms are those of the Dukedoms of Brunswick and Lüneburg impaled (i.e. side by side). The blue over yellow flag is still very much used today, privately and on official buildings in recognition of their historic significance.

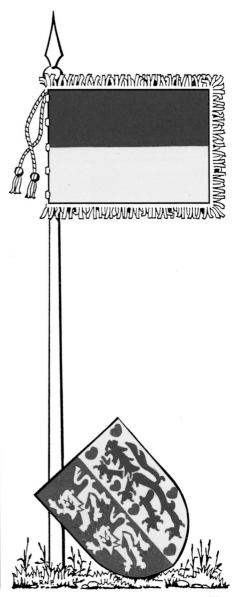

OLDENBURG

The Counts of Oldenburg became independent in 1180 to rule an area by the North Sea coast at the mouth of the Weser. Although its lands were small in extent, the House of Oldenburg has been the origin of sovereigns of Norway, Denmark, Sweden, Russia and Greece.

In the 17th century Oldenburg became a possession of the Danish crown but regained its independence in 1773. In the 19th century Oldenburg became a political pawn in the complicated question of the Schleswig-Holstein succession, about which Lord Palmerston is reputed to have said that only three people had ever fully understood it — the Prince Consort (who was dead), a German professor of history (who had gone mad), and himself (who had forgotten)!

Today, as a result of the post-war reorganisation of Germany, Oldenburg is incorporated in the west German federal *Land* of Lower Saxony, within which it retains a measure of identity.

The arms are ancient. The traditional blue flag with a red cross, which dates from the late 18th century, is still proudly flown from public buildings in Oldenburg.

Df [> Af]

SCHAUMBERG-LIPPE

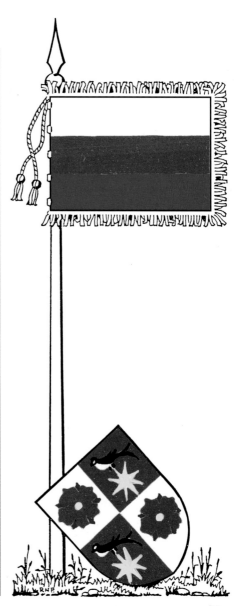

The smallest of the German states prior to the end of the Second World War, Schaumberg-Lippe lies on the east bank of the Weser.

Typical of the several hundred small states which made up the old Holy Roman Empire, it survived the dissolution of that venerable, if ramshackle, institution, and Napoleon's subsequent restructuring of Germany, to be admitted as a sovereign principality to the Confederation of the Rhine in 1807. It joined the Kaiser's German Empire (Reich) in 1871.

After the fall of the Kaiser in the revolution of 1918, Schaumberg-Lippe became a free state with a democratic republican constitution from 1922. In 1946 it was incorporated within the new *Land Niedersachsen* (Lower Saxony).

Some politicians have advocated merging *Länder* to form larger units. The seven German territories described so far, together with Westphalia, do in fact form a coherent ethnic unit which approximates with the great 10th century Saxon duchy. An enlarged Lower Saxony could therefore emerge with the historic territories as autonomous provinces.

The quartered arms of Schaumberg-Lippe carry the charges of the red rose of Lippe and the martlet and star of Schaumberg. The flag is that used by the formerly autonomous state, and although autonomy no longer obtains, it is still flown from public buildings and by private citizens as an expression of national identity.

WESTPHALIA

The prosperous land of North Rhine-Westphalia is the most populous state in Germany. It was a somewhat artificial creation arising out of the post-war reorganisation of Germany. Previously, under the 1815 Congress of Vienna, Prussia had absorbed Westphalia and the Duchy of the Lower Rhine, to become separate provinces of the German Empire.

The portion of the state which forms Westphalia was originally a province of the old duchy of Saxony. The territory includes the Ruhr Valley, heartland of Germany's industrial might. In 1945 Düsseldorf, formerly capital of the small state of Berg, became *Land* capital of the new state. Around the same time the northern portion of Westphalia was incorporated into Lower Saxony.

The Rhineland and Westphalia-Lippe each have separate regional leagues with seats respectively in Cologne and Münster. The duties covered by these leagues include traffic, cultural affairs and welfare. The Rhineland/Westphalia boundary corresponds to the old ethnic boundary between Franks of Middle German speech and Low-German-speaking Saxons.

It is open to speculation whether a more radical division of the two territories is a practical political proposition, but as the process of German unification unfolds, opportunities for adjustment to state boundaries may emerge in the western as well as eastern parts of Germany.

The traditional arms of Westphalia, dating from the Middle Ages, share the prancing Saxon horse with Hanover and with the modern state of Lower Saxony. The flag is that originally used by Westphalia during the Napoleonic Wars.

Df [> Af]

RHINELAND

Franks have occupied the fecund basin of the great Rhine waterway and its tributaries since the third century AD. The history of the area is complex but, before the dissolution of Prussia, the term Rhineland was used to designate the Prussian *Rhein-provinz* together with adjacent territories.

Among the important towns of the Rhineland are the ancient fortress and trading centre of Cologne, dating from Roman times, Aachen, Charlemagne's capital, and Bonn, the provisional post-war federal capital of West Germany.

After the Second World War the Rhineland was split between the new states of North Rhine-Westphalia and of Rhineland Palatinate. Under this arrangement, each territory has prospered.

Whether or not a formal division of North Rhine-Westphalia into its traditional ethnic components is politically likely, is hard to speculate. Should this occur, the possibility would emerge of creating a new reunified Rhineland by incorporating a portion of the Rhineland Palatinate or indeed a wider merger with the other Frankish *Länder* of Hesse, Rhineland Palatinate and Saarland.

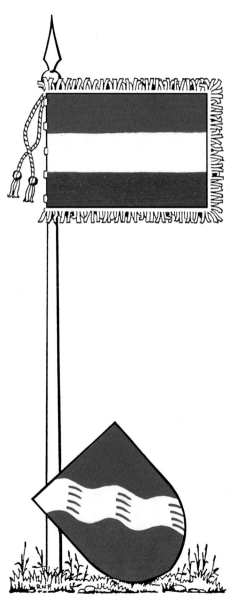

The arms illustrated formed an inescutcheon on the imperial eagle of the former Duchy of the Lower Rhine, and are a component of the arms of the Land of North Rhine-Westphalia. The flag was used by the separatist movement in the Rhineland after the First World War, and was subsequently adopted by the Land of Rhineland Westphalia.

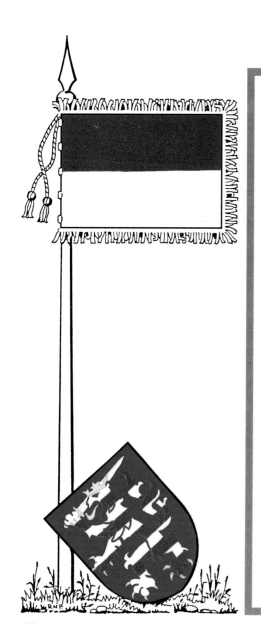

HESSE

The Hessians are a Frankish people who were Christianised in the 8th century. They settled in the territory which became known as Hesse. It lies between the Rhenish uplands in the west and the Thuringian forest in the east.

Hesse has ancient dynastic associations with Thuringia. In 1265 Henry of Brabant became the first Landgrave of Hesse, an inheritance later to be subdivided into a number of noble lines, of which Hesse-Kassel and Hesse-Darmstadt survive to this day.

In the 16th century, under Philip I, a fervent supporter of Martin Luther, Hesse became an early centre for Protestantism in the German Reformation. The 18th century Landgraves of Hesse were noted for their construction of lavish baroque palaces. This extravagance necessitated the sale of Hessian subjects as mercenary soldiers.

In 1945 most of the former territories of Hesse-Kassel, Hesse-Darmstadt and Nassau were merged to form the present West German *Land* of Greater Hesse (*Gross Hessen*, subsequently called *Hessen*).

The largest city, and former capital of the great 10th century duchy of Franconia, is Frankfurt am Main, a leading German commercial centre, and home of the Bundesbank, Europe's premier financial institution.

The distinctive arms originated in the 13th century. Today the flag in official use in Hesse is often charged with the arms (without the sword).

Af

PALATINATE

This warm dry Rhine Valley land has been cultivated since Neolithic times and was an early place of settlement for German peoples.

In 1214 Emperor Frederick II created Otto Wittlesbach Count Palatine, originally a title applied to an official with special powers derived from the imperial palace. Dynastically the Palatinate maintained a strong link with Bavaria through the centuries. The town of Mainz became one of the most important in medieval Germany.

After the re-organisation of Germany at the end of the Second World War Mainz was chosen as capital of the new *Land* of Rhineland-Palatinate, which was assembled from the Palatinate, Rhine-Hesse and much of the Rhenish uplands, mainly to create a zone of occupation for the French.

It was predicted at the time that, as an artificial political unit, the Rhineland Palatinate would be divided among surrounding *Länder*. This has not thus far happened and the new *Land* has prospered. If there were, however, to be a reorganisation of the disposition of the federal *Länder*, it has been suggested that a new Frankish state could emerge perhaps with the Palatinate as one of its autonomous provinces.

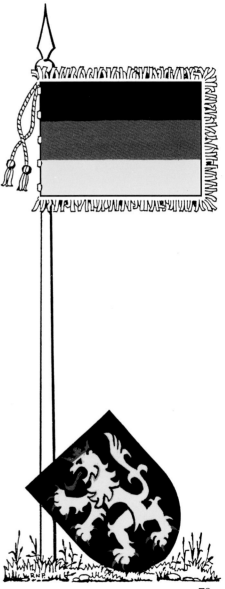

The ancient arms of the Palatinate are a gold lion with red crown, tongue and claws on a black field. The flag takes its colours from the coat of arms and are the same as those for the Federal Republic of Germany. The current flag of Rhineland-Palatinate has a crowned coat of arms in the canton which, besides the lion of the Palatinate, carries a red cross of Kur-Trier and a white wheel on a red ground of Kur-Mainz.

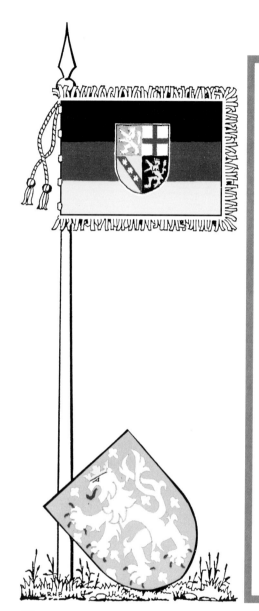

SAARLAND

A German-speaking area since olden times, bounded on the east by Luxemburg and to the south by France, Saarland has from time to time in recent centuries come under French influence.

After Germany's defeat in the Great War, the rich Saar coal mines were ceded to France in reparation for war damage. In 1920, the Saar was placed under a governing commission of the League of Nations for fifteen years, after which time a plebiscite on the territory's future was to be held.

In the event, the 1935 plebiscite resulted in an overwhelming (90%) vote for a return to Germany. The territory and its mines were accordingly handed back.

Again in 1945 after the Second World War, the Saar was occupied by France, and this time given autonomous status under French control. By the mid 1950s, however, this status was the subject of political dispute, and in 1959, Saarland once more returned to Germany as the tenth *Land* of the Federal Republic, with its capital in Saarbrücken.

If, as alluded to in the previous three pages, suggested mergers of the *Länder* take place, Saarland's Frankish population may seek closer political links with its Frankish neighbours. In such an event it is to be hoped that the autonomy and identity of Saarland and the other historic components are maintained.

The arms shown here are those of the County of Saarbrücken. The official Land flag adopted in 1956, is a version of the federal flag charged with a shield, the quarters of which represent Saarbrücken, Kur-Trier (the cross), Lorraine, and Kur-Palatinate.

Af

SWABIA

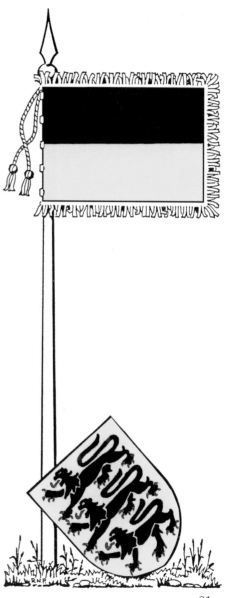

This southern German land has been settled and cultivated since pre-Roman times by Germanic Alemanni, or Swabians, from whom in the 9th century the ancient Duchy of Swabia took its name. One of the great Carolingian duchies, Swabia eventually failed in the early 13th century.

From medieval times two dynastic houses grew to dominate Swabia, evolving respectively into the Kingdom of Württemberg and the Duchy of Baden. The area prospered as the focus for the Swabian League of Cities in the 14th century, which in the South German War of the Cities (1377–85) vanquished Count Eberhard of Württemberg.

The late 18th century witnessed a great migration of Swabian people to Galicia (east Poland) and Bukovina (south Ukraine) thereby reinforcing earlier German settlement in eastern Europe. In 1870/71, Württemberg and Baden each became part of the German Empire.

In 1952, with the reorganisation of Germany after the Second World War, a new *Land* of Baden-Württemberg, was created in Swabia out of the separate prewar *Länder* of Baden and Württemberg and the small Prussian province of Hohenzollern. Stuttgart, a major centre of banking, commerce and administration, became the *Land* capital.

The arms originate with the Hohenstaufen emperors and the ancient Duchy of Swabia. Today the flag of Baden-Württemberg is frequently seen charged with the arms (but without the red forepaws).

Af

BAVARIA

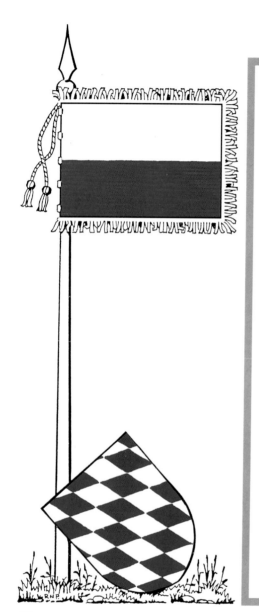

The earliest known inhabitants were Celts, whose language was replaced by German during the Dark Ages. German has remained the tongue of the Bavarians ever since.

Conquered by Charlemagne at the end of the 8th century, Bavaria has been associated with the House of Wittlesbach since 1180. Of the many notable Wittlesbach rulers, perhaps the most eccentric was the mad King Ludwig II (1864–1886), a patron of Wagner, and builder of fantastic romantic castles such as Neuschwanstein, an inspiration behind Walt Disney's Magic Kingdom.

The family are still dukes in Bavaria, the old monarchy having been dissolved at the end of the First World War.

Bavaria was always the most independent of the great German duchies. This characteristic remains to this day in the Free State of Bavaria, largest of the modern German *Länder*, in which a high level of prosperity obtains. In contrast to the prevalence of Protestantism in much of northern Germany, the Bavarians adhere, mainly, to the Roman Catholic faith. The *Land* capital is Munich.

The striking 12th century arms of Bavaria — 'paly bendy argent and azure' — used by the present-day Bavarian state, are originally those of the House of Wittlesbach. The flag generally used in Bavaria is the white over blue bi-colour, although, strictly speaking, the official version is a lozengy banner of the arms. In centuries past, other variants have been flown — mainly blue and white stripes.

BERLIN

Medieval Berlin began as two modest settlements — Kolln, an island in the Spree (first mentioned in 1237), and Berlin itself, to the east across the river some years later.

It was not till 1415, when Berlin was chosen as residence of the Hohenzollern rulers of Brandenburg, that the town began to grow in significance. This trend was re-inforced by the rise of Brandenburg-Prussia to predominance within a united Germany. In 1700 there were still fewer than 29,000 inhabitants. By 1943 the figure had reached 4.3 million.

In 1945, war and defeat reduced much of Berlin to rubble. The occupying forces divided the city into four sectors of which in 1948 the Soviet sector became East Berlin, while the American, British and French sectors became West Berlin. West Berlin thus became an enclave of West Germany completely surrounded by the politically distinct Communist East Germany.

In 1948, for almost a year, West Berlin was blockaded by the East German authorities and every item of food and fuel had to be flown in by the 'Berlin air-lift'. The blockade failed and West Berlin subsequently prospered under Allied control.

To halt the westward flood of refugees, the GDR (East German) authorities constructed the infamous Berlin Wall in 1961, a stark symbol of a divided Europe. Its removal was a cherished aim realised in 1989 with the collapse of the Communist government in the GDR. The reunited Berlin was thereafter set to regain its status as capital of unified Germany.

The bear coat of arms dates from about 1200 and the flag was adopted in 1912.

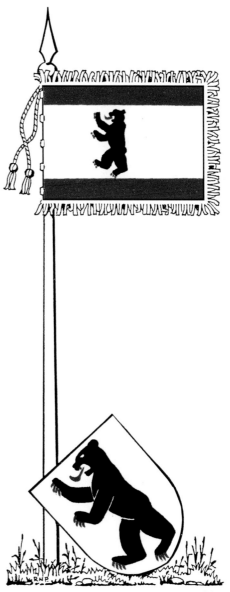

BRANDENBURG

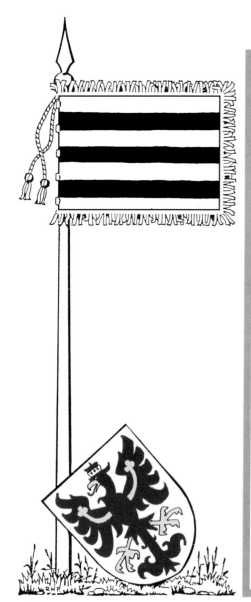

In the 12th century the Lords of the Marches, with crusading zeal, pushed the north-eastern boundary of Germany eastwards into Slav territory. This new area of settlement became the North Mark, later Brandenburg and springboard for further eastwards colonisation by German people.

In time Brandenburg, through the house of Hohenzollern, expanded to control a powerful and extensive empire. By the outbreak of the First World War in 1914, Brandenburg-Prussia stretched from the Dutch border in the west to East Prussia and Memel in the east, containing some 60% of Germany's inhabitants.

In 1945 Brandenburg-Prussia was dismembered: a post-war *Land* of Brandenburg was created, within the Soviet Zone of occupation, to correspond fairly closely with the original North Mark. The wheel had come full circle. In 1952, however, the East German *Länder* were abolished and the GDR was reorganised into districts of which Brandenburg constituted Cottbus, Frankfurt and Potsdam.

With the collapse of the corrupt East German Communist government in 1989, the return of democracy and the unification of the two Germanies, the *Land* of Brandenburg was re-established in 1990 as one of the five east German federal *Länder* covering the territory of the former GDR.

The red eagle in the arms of Brandenburg carries a gold kleestengel very characteristic of German heraldry. The flag dates back to olden times.

MECKLENBURG

This Baltic coast *Land*, lying south-east of Denmark, was occupied from the 6th century by Slav peoples. Mecklenburg became increasingly Germanised from around the 10th century but the rulers remained of Slav origin, a feature unique in Germany.

The speech of Mecklenburg, like that of other parts of north Germany, has for many centuries been Low German, while in modern times, High German has been the official language.

As the Second World War ended, Mecklenburg fell within the Soviet Zone of occupation and in 1945 the *Land* of Mecklenburg was extended to include the western parts of Pomerania which had not been seized by the Poles.

In common with the other East German *Länder*, *Land Mecklenburg Vorpommern* was abolished and divided into the newly formed districts of Rostock, Schwerin and Neubrandenburg. With the German unification in 1990, the re-establishment of Mecklenburg as a *Land* became a reality once more.

As a function of Germany's federal system of government, the restoration, in east Germany, of the post-war *Länder* was a fundamental element in the rebuilding of democracy within formerly Communist territory. The evolution of the recently enlarged Germany may, in time, see amalgamations creating a smaller number of larger *Länder*, but with traditional territories retaining their identity and autonomy.

The arms of Mecklenburg, a bull's head, sometimes shown with a ring in its mouth, is of medieval origin. The flag is traditional.

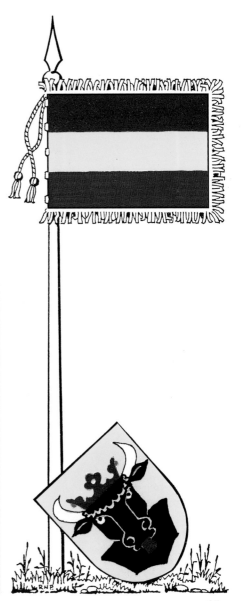

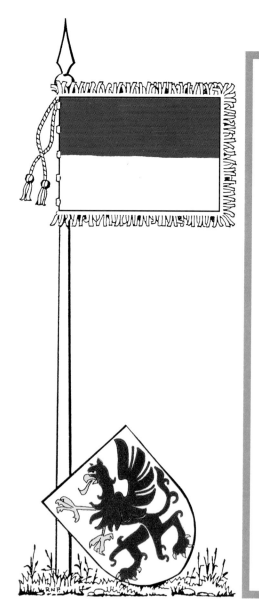

POMERANIA

This flat region of the Baltic south coast and its hinterland stretched from the Lower Vistula to Stralsund and the Island of Rügen. The original Slavic name 'Pomorze' means 'along the sea'. The area was inhabited almost entirely by Slavs until the 13th century.

From that time, however, the country was opened up to German immigrants, which resulted in a gradual Germanisation of firstly the towns and then the rural nobility.

From 1773 most of Pomerania came under German (Prussian) control (parts of Vor-Pommern were in Swedish hands until 1815). During the period of German occupation, however, much of the rural population remained Slav (Polish) in speech.

After 1945, with the dismemberment of Germany following its defeat in the Second World War, eastern Pomerania (east of the Oder) plus the city of Stettin (Polish 'Szczecin') became part of the reconstituted post-war Poland. The remainder of western Pomerania was incorporated into the (Communist) German Democratic Republic.

The rebirth of democracy in the eastern part of Germany allowed West Pomerania and Mecklenburg together to form a single *Land*. With its distinct history and identity, West Pomerania may find the opportunity to develop a more autonomous existence, if Germany's federal structure is reorganised along the lines alluded to in previous pages.

The red griffon on the arms was the emblem of the Dukes of Pomerania and has been in more or less continuous use as a Pomeranian symbol since at least the 14th century. The flag is that of the Prussian province of Pommern.

D [> Af]

THURINGIA

The Thuringians were one of the original Germanic tribes distinct from the other German peoples such as the Franks, Saxons and Bavarians. In the time of Charlemagne their area of settlement west of the River Saale formed a border with the Slavs.

In their later history the Thuringian principalities gave the world a brilliant literary and intellectual legacy through the works of men like Goethe, Schiller and Luther. The area also developed a tradition of metal working and manufacturing which continues to this day.

Although the seven small Thuringian principalities remained independent of Prussia, they joined the German customs union in 1834. They were eventually amalgamated in 1919 to form a new *Land Thuringen*. At the end of the Second World War Thuringia fell within the Soviet Zone and in common with the other reconstituted East German *Länder* was abolished as a political unit in 1952.

For nearly four decades Thuringian identity was suppressed by the Communists, but with the collapse of the Communist regime in East Germany, it re-emerged to fuel the re-establishment of the Thuringian state.

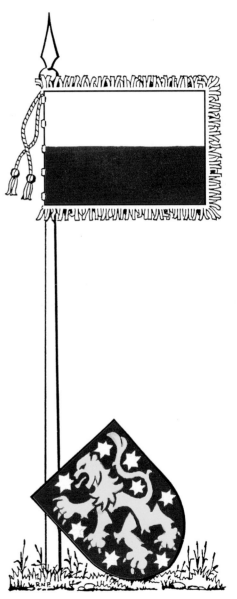

A red shield with seven silver six-pointed stars (representing the formerly independent principalities) formed the new arms created in 1921 for the then recently constituted Land Thuringen. In 1945 a further star and a gold lion were added as shown to form the arms of the temporarily reconstituted post-war state. A variant of this bearing a striped lion (see Hesse) has now been adopted together with the white over red bi-colour flag.

SAXONY

After the great tribal migrations around the 5th century the pagan Saxons, a Germanic people, had settled a large part of north-western Germany. Many even sailed west with other Germanic tribes to settle in England.

By the 10th century, Saxony formed one of the five great duchies of Germany. After centuries of dynastic sub-division, Saxony became a kingdom in 1806 but ceded a large northern tract to become a province of Prussia. In common with other German rulers, the king was compelled to abdicate in 1918 and Saxony became a federal *Land*.

It so remained, even for a time during the period of Soviet occupation, until split into the new East German districts of Leipzig, Chemnitz (Karl Marx Stadt) and Dresden. The former and separate Prussian province of Saxony became the separate *Land* Saxony-Anhalt in 1945. Like its neighbour, it was similarly split in 1952 to form the districts of Magdeburg and Halle.

Following the collapse of the Communist government, Saxony and Saxony-Anhalt were re-established as separate federal *Länder*. Re-amalgamation of the two territories may be a future possibility. There is a small and long-standing minority of Sorbs whose Slavic language is protected.

The arms of Saxony are said to result from the draping of Emperor Barbarossa's chaplet of rue over the black and gold shield of Duke Bernard of Ascania. The flag is that of the old kingdom and, after decades of suppression by the Communists, re-emerged as a focus of nationality in pro-democracy demonstrations in Leipzig and other Saxon centres in 1989.

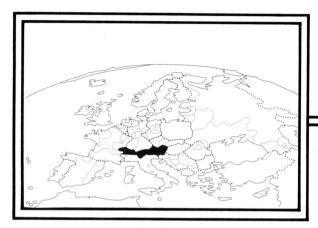

62 Switzerland   63 Austria
64 Liechtenstein   65 Tyrol

Europe's Backbone
THE ALPINE LANDS

The mountain range of the Alps is the backbone of Europe. They form a natural barrier, containing Europe's highest peaks and stretch 780 miles from the south of France to Vienna. Until the Dark Ages, the inhabitants of much of the territory adjacent to the Alps were Celts. For almost two millennia, however, the Alpine watershed has corresponded closely with the major linguistic divide, very effectively separating Germanic northern Europe from the Latin south.

The Alpine waters, swollen by melting snow, are today a major source of hydro-electric power. They flow in all directions to give birth to the great river and communication systems of the Rhine, Danube, Rhône and Po.

There are a number of passes through the Alps; each has had its role in European history, and has through the centuries enriched those who controlled them.

Despite their relatively inhospitable terrain and poverty of industrial resources, the Alpine lands are today among Europe's most prosperous economies. The Alps themselves have become a massive tourist playground, summer and winter. They are also of great ecological importance as the habitat for many rare species of flora and fauna.

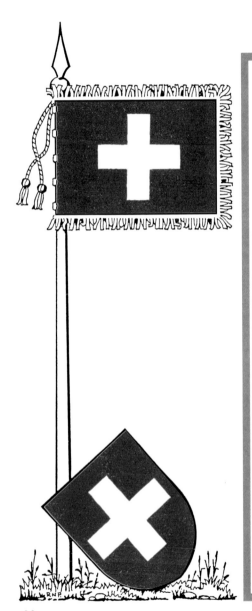

SWITZERLAND

This fiercely independent Europe in miniature dates back to 1291 when three independent cantons, or provinces, around Lake Lucerne (Uri, Schwyz and Unterwalden) organised themselves into the Swiss Confederation, run ever since on federal and democratic lines.

Gradually, over the centuries, other cantons joined the confederation until today their number is 26. Each has a large degree of autonomy, leaving relatively few, but essential, powers to the federal government — defence, currency, customs, posts etc. Despite strong democratic credentials, women do not yet have the vote in some cantons.

Although its population is only around five million, Switzerland has become one of Europe's most prosperous countries with an international standing out of all proportion to its small size.

This can be attributed to a number of factors including a policy of neutrality, thereby avoiding costly involvement in war, a democratic tradition which has prevented the emergence of a landed aristocracy, and political independence which has permitted the Swiss to grasp any economic opportunity to their collective advantage.

The multilingual Swiss have long recognised the rights of people to their own religion and language. Three official languages are recognised — German (three-quarters of the population), French and Italian. Romansch has the status of national language.

The white cross on a red ground has been known as an emblem of Switzerland since 1339, although the arms were officially adopted only as recently as 1941. The flag shown is the merchant flag; the commonly used federal flag is identical but square.

AUSTRIA

Austria began modestly as Ostmark, a frontier province of Germany which, in the 10th century, was able to halt the westward advance of the feared heathen Magyar (Hungarian) menace.

The Austrian domain gradually expanded over the centuries, particularly under the illustrious Habsburg line. By 1519 Charles I of Austria was ruler of Spain, Burgundy, The Netherlands, Austria and, as Holy Roman Emperor, overlord of Germany.

By the 17th century the energies of Austria were again directed eastwards; this time against the Turks who had conquered most of the Balkans (south-eastern Europe). By the end of that century, as a result of Austria's efforts, almost all of Hungary and Croatia were in Habsburg hands.

By the 19th century, although Austria had lost her western possessions, the mighty Austro-Hungarian Empire dominated east central Europe. To satisfy Magyar demands for autonomy the Empire was transformed into a dual monarchy under the 'Ausgleich', or compromise, of 1867.

It all ended with the close of the First World War. The struggle for self-determination of the Empire's disparate peoples was vindicated in the peace terms of 1918. The new states of Yugoslavia, Czechoslovakia and Poland were created — returning Austria to something like its original size. The language of Austria is German, although there is a small Slovene minority.

The arms of Austria are very ancient, dating back to 1200 or earlier. A banner of the arms is known to have existed in 1230. The flag was first officially used as a war ensign in 1786.

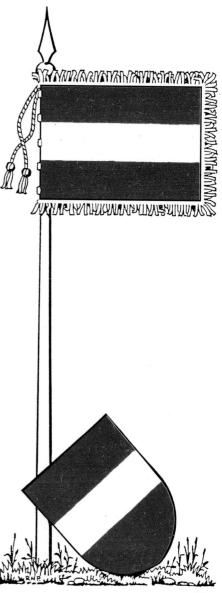

LIECHTENSTEIN

This micro state, capital Vaduz, with a population of only 20,000, covers just 62 square miles between Switzerland and Austria. In 1719 the lordships of Vaduz and Schellenburg were created an independent principality under the Holy Roman Empire and given the name of Liechtenstein.

With the break-up of the Empire, the principality survived as a member of the German Confederation. It entered into a customs union with Austria in 1852, became independent in 1866 and entered a customs and postal union with Switzerland in 1924. All this happened under the rule of Prince John II, who ruled Liechtenstein until 1929. His reign of 71 years is a European record!

Today the independent Principality of Liechtenstein is said to be Europe's most prosperous state. Its main industries are banking, precision instruments, tourism and false teeth manufacture. The language is German and the religion Roman Catholicism.

The arms are those of the state and house of Liechtenstein. The blue and red on the flag are said to represent the sky and the evening hearth fires. The crown is that of a prince of the Holy Roman Empire.

TYROL

This Alpine country has been closely associated with Austria since the Middle Ages. With the break-up of the Austro-Hungarian Empire at the close of the First World War, the long-established unity of the Tyrol was destroyed: the portion south of the Alpine watershed was arbitrarily detached from Austria and transferred to the Italian state, forming the new province of Trentino-Alto Adige.

Although the population of the area was overwhelmingly German in speech and culture, Mussolini's then new Fascist regime embarked upon a ruthless and systematic programme of Italianisation.

The process included the encouragement of ethnic Italian in-migration, job discrimination against German speakers and obligatory Italianisation of most aspects of public and private life including education, place and personal names, and even the wording of gravestones!

The return to democracy after the end of the Second World War saw the rights of South Tyrol's German population restored in full. The area is now in many respects a model of enlightened linguistic policy, which facilitates the enjoyment of a common Tyrolean culture across a state boundary.

Austrian Tyrol is wholly German. In South Tyrol, German speakers form about 70% of the population. In addition to the Italian community, there is also a Ladino minority who are said to be descended from the original Celtic inhabitants of the area.

The arms of Tyrol date from about 1200 and the flag is one of several variants used over the centuries.

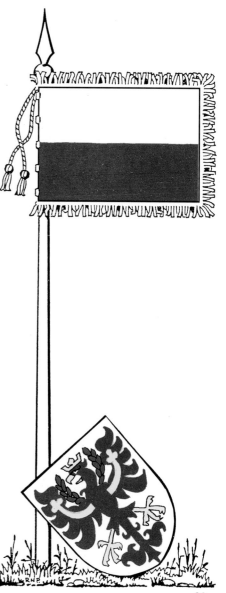

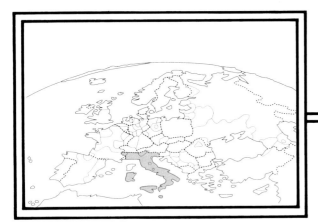

66 Italy 67 Sardinia 68 Aosta
69 Venice 70 Friuli 71 Vatican
72 San Marino 73 Malta

Rome's Legacy
THE ITALIAN PENINSULA

Migration of Indo-European peoples into the Italian peninsula began around 2000 BC and continued for a thousand years. From among these people, the Etruscans emerged to flourish between the Arno and Tiber rivers. In the 6th century BC this gifted race was overthrown by the new and growing republican Rome. By 264 BC, all Italy, south of Cisalpine Gaul, was unified under a multi-cultural confederation, whose members were either incorporated within, or allied with, the Roman state. Roman citizenship was extended to all Italy by 90 BC. When the Roman republic fell in 44 BC, an Empire was launched, which by AD 180 extended from Spain to the Euphrates river, and from Britain to Africa. It has been said that this mighty structure's influence has never been surpassed by any other human organisation.

The Latin language remains the basis of the speech of over half a billion people today. The Roman alphabet is in almost universal use. Roman law, architecture, road building etc. remain the foundation of modern practice. The Christian religion, which the Romans made official by grafting it on to their own *Sol Invictus* cult, became the catalyst for European evolution.

It has to be said that humanity also lost a great deal in the Romanisation process — the subjugation of women, slavery, corruption, the concept of imagined racial and cultural superiority and the exploitative abuse of the environment all represent the darker side of Rome's legacy. As with all empires, the internal seeds of Rome's ultimate destruction became manifest as dissipation, injustice and maladministration accelerated. The 'barbarian' invasions of the 4th and 5th centuries delivered the *coup de grâce*.

ITALY

After the fall of Rome, Italy became fragmented and was to remain so for centuries. Despite this, its Roman and Christian heritage gave the various independent principalities a continuing prestige.

From the 13th to 16th centuries, Italy was Europe's undoubted cultural centre. There the Renaissance revolutionised scientific and artistic thought, thereby creating the conditions for the evolution of the modern world. This process remains one of the highest achievements in human endeavour.

The Italian unification movement took place in the 19th century, largely through the efforts of the House of Savoy, the rulers of the northern Italian state of Piedmont. By 1861 they succeeded in uniting most of Italy under their king Victor Emmanuel II. Annexation of Venetia in 1866 and Papal Rome in 1870 marked the complete unification of the Italian nation state as a monarchy.

Fascism spread in Italy under Benito Mussolini but was eventually crushed in 1943. In 1946 a republic was proclaimed and Italy, as a founder member of the European Community, has since developed as one of the most dynamic economies in Europe.

The Italian language is universally spoken throughout Italy, Sardinia and parts of Switzerland. There are Greek, Albanian, Slovene, Croatian, Rom, Occitan, Friulian, Ladino, Franco-Provençal, Sard and German-speaking communities, of which only the Germans and Ladinos have linguistic rights.

The flag is a variation of the French tricolour dating from the end of the 18th century. It became the national flag in 1861. The arms (not currently in use) are those of the House of Savoy.

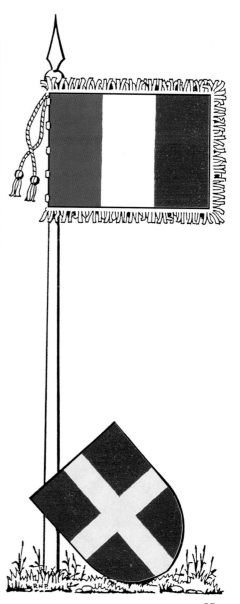

SARDINIA

This large Mediterranean island, 12 km south of Corsica and 200 km west of the Italian peninsula, has belonged successively to the Romans, Vandals, Byzantines, Arabs, Pisa and Genoa. The house of Aragon gained control from 1326, leading to Spanish domination until 1708, when Sardinia passed to Austria.

In 1720 the Kingdom of Sardinia was ceded to the House of Savoy which also ruled Piedmont in northern Italy. During the Napoleonic wars, Piedmont was annexed by France, but after the war the Kingdom of Sardinia regained its mainland territories which it expanded through the 19th century to include almost all of Italy. From 1861 Sardinia became part of the united Italian state. Today as a semi-autonomous region, with a population of 1.6 million, it has its capital in Cagliari.

The Sard language (*Sardo*) is the most similar to vulgar Latin of all the Romance languages. There are several dialects, little literature, and no standard form. Nine per cent speak Sard exclusively and 80% are bilingual. There are also 20,000 people in the city of Alghero who speak or understand Catalan.

For some years there has been conflict between the Regional Government, seeking to establish equal rights for Sard (but not Catalan), and the Central Government who oppose these moves. A number of local but unco-ordinated initiatives have been undertaken to promote teaching of Sard, broadcasting etc.

The arms and flag, which are commonly used, combine severed Moors' heads (see Corsica) with the red cross of Genoa.

A

VALLE D'AOSTA

This Alpine valley province of north-west Italy occupies the upper basin of the Dora Baltea river and commands the Great and Little St. Bernard Passes. The area was a stronghold of the Salassi, a Celtic tribe subdued by the Romans in 25 BC.

In early medieval times the Valle d'Aosta formed part of the great Burgundian and Frankish kingdoms. Later it came under a series of rulers until it was acquired by the Counts of Savoy in the 11th century.

Historical fate selected the House of Savoy to be the vehicle for Italy's unification in the 19th century. The Valle d'Aosta was incorporated within Italy as an integral part of this process.

70,000 out of a total of 110,000 inhabitants speak Franco-Provençal. In recognition of this, the Valle d'Aosta was created an autonomous region in 1945. It is the French language, however, which receives legal protection, rather than Franco-Provençal, which still has no legal status. The 20,000 Franco-Provençals who live in adjacent provinces of Italy have even less recognition.

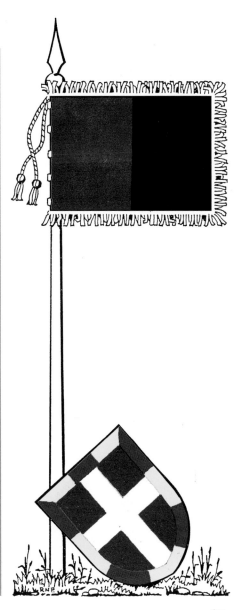

The arms of the Valle d'Aosta are a differenced version of the arms of Savoy (and therefore Italy). The flag has been in use as a symbol of autonomy for some decades.

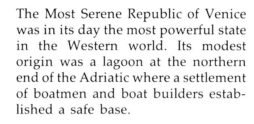

The Most Serene Republic of Venice was in its day the most powerful state in the Western world. Its modest origin was a lagoon at the northern end of the Adriatic where a settlement of boatmen and boat builders established a safe base.

The small community prospered on the salt trade. In the 7th century they founded the City of Venice, whose republican government was to last for 1000 years. The city moved in the 11th century to its present island location on the Rialto.

By the 16th century Venice dominated European trade through control of an extensive maritime empire in the eastern Mediterranean and the Black Sea. Venice was at the height of its prestige and led Europe in learning, art and fashion. Marco Polo, Titian, Bellini, Vivaldi and Casanova were all sons of Venice. By this time the city state had also expanded onto the mainland.

A gradual decline set in: first with the loss of the Empire to the Turks, then through a process of internal dissipation. Venice eventually fell to Napoleon and then for a time became an Austrian possession. With the reunification of Italy Venice was incorporated into the Italian state.

Venice remains a unique architectural gem of world importance but is in peril of disintegration unless a massive programme of protection and restoration is completed quickly. Work is now in hand but would be aided by giving Venice special autonomous status as a permanent European city of culture.

The distinctive arms and flag carry the winged lion of St. Mark, the patron saint of Venice.

D > A

FRIULI

In its strategic location as the meeting place of Latins, Slavs and Germans, at the head of the Adriatic, the Friulian patriarchal state was, for about three and a half centuries, one of the grandest and most refined political organisations of the Middle Ages. Annexed in 1420 to the Venetian Republic, and later falling under Austrian hegemony, Friuli was finally incorporated into the Italian state after the First World War.

The Latin-based Friulian language with its strong Celtic substratum is spoken by over 500,000 people. It is under threat, suffers official oppression and is generally forbidden as a teaching medium in schools, although some use has been made of it in nursery schools. There is, however, a limited amount of publishing and broadcasting.

In contrast, the related Ladino language, spoken by about 30,000 people in the Trentino-South Tyrol region has much greater official recognition and support, particularly in Bolzano where the language is virtually on a par with Italian.

Also within the Friuli-Venezia Giulia region are about 150,000 Slovenes, mainly along the border with Yugoslavia. There is official antipathy to any display of Slovene ethnicity because of supposed links with the Communist regime in Yugoslavia.

The recovery effort following the earthquake of 1976 turned disaster into a renewed sense of Friulan consciousness. Hopefully improved cultural and linguistic rights and greater political autonomy will follow.

The arms date back to the time of the independent patriarchal state and the flag carries the livery colours of the arms.

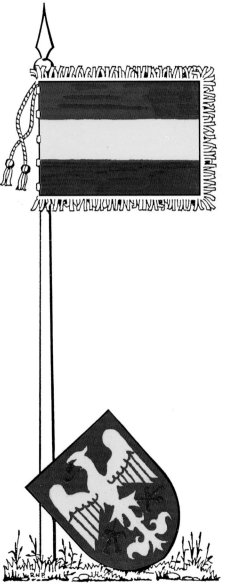

D > A or I

THE VATICAN CITY

The Papal states were founded in AD 754 as a political possession of the Catholic Church of Rome. These states lasted for over 1000 years until extinguished in 1870 by the unification of Italy. The Pontif refused thereafter to emerge from the Vatican until his sovereignty was again recognised. As a result of the Lateran Treaty, the Vatican City was once more recognised as an independent sovereign state in 1929.

The Vatican City, characterised by its quaint streets and Swiss Guards in 16th century uniform, earns revenue from tourism and the sale of postage stamps. The languages of the Vatican are Latin and Italian.

This tiny remnant of the once extensive Papal States has only some 800 residents but is, nevertheless, the location of the world's largest church, the offices of the Holy See and the Curia (the government of the Roman Catholic Church). For those reasons this micro state has an international influence out of all proportion to its size.

The keys featured in the arms and flag signify the authority conferred by Christ on the Apostle Peter in Matthew XVI, 19. The triple tiara is another emblem of Papal authority. Both date back to the 13th century. The red field of the arms has been the colour for the Catholic Church since medieval times. The yellow and white of the flag, which represent the gold and silver keys of St. Peter, date from 1825.

SAN MARINO

'The Most Serene Republic of San Marino', a mountain micro state situated just inland from the Adriatic town of Rimini, is totally surrounded by Italian territory. It has been an independent republic since AD 885, although tradition states that it was founded as early as AD 301 by St. Marinus as a refuge for those fleeing religious or political persecution.

Within San Marino's 38 square miles the population of about 15,000 Sammarinesi speak Italian and use Italian currency, although the republic issues its own stamps.

The RSM, as the republic is known, is governed by a sixty-member Grand Council (Parliament) and a ten-man Congress of State. Two Captains Regent, elected from the Grand Council for terms of six months, act as Heads of State. The republic has no armed forces apart from a ceremonial platoon of crossbowmen and has been an active member of the non-aligned movement.

Wheat, livestock and wine are the traditional products but nowadays tourism also forms an appreciable component of the economy.

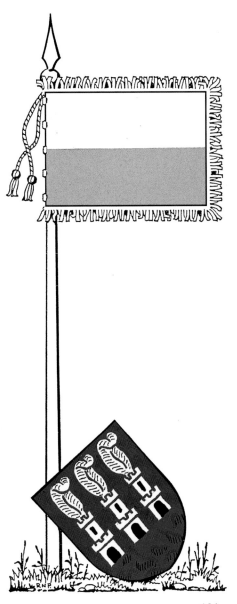

The motif of three towers surmounted by ostrich feathers dates back to at least the 14th century. They make reference to the three towers, Montale, Cesta, and Guaita of the walled city of San Marino. The flag was adopted around 1797 using the main colours of the arms.

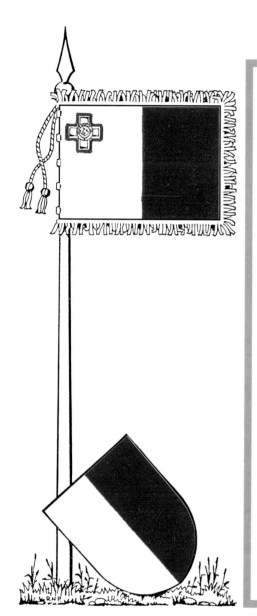

MALTA

In 218 BC the Phoenician islands of Malta, Gozo and Comino fell to the Romans. In AD 60 St. Paul and St. Luke were shipwrecked in the archipelago. Their preaching of the Gospel during that winter introduced Christianity to the islands and led to the conversion of Publius, the Roman governor, who became the first Bishop of Malta.

The Maltese have adhered tenaciously to Christianity ever since, despite two centuries of Arab occupation. The Arabs' permanent legacy is the (Semitic) Malti language, still universally spoken by all Maltese citizens.

In early medieval times Malta was ruled at various times by French, Sicilian and Spanish nobles. By the 15th century a measure of home rule was achieved under an administration called the Universita. Members of the Order of St. John arrived in 1530 and stayed until expelled by Napoleon at the end of the 18th century. The islands came under British rule from 1814.

Over the centuries Malta has had its share of struggle, from the terrible Turkish siege of 1565 to the siege of 1942, both of which Malta survived. In the latter case, to honour the islanders' courage, they were collectively awarded Britain's highest civilian honour — the George Cross.

In 1964 Malta became an independent republic.

The arms are said to date from 1190. They also feature the colours of the Knights of St. John, whose Maltese Cross features on the country's ensign. A bi-colour banner of the arms has however been used since olden times and is the official flag of the republic, nowadays augmented by a George Cross in canton.

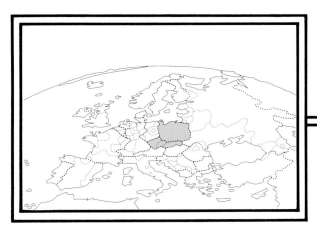

74 Poland   75 Bohemia
76 Moravia   77 Slovakia

The Western Slavs
POLAND & CZECHOSLOVAKIA

As a result of the great European tribal migrations which took place during the early centuries of the Dark Ages, the Slavs came to occupy vast tracts of land throughout eastern Europe.

In time the original Slav language of these Indo-European peoples diverged into three major sub-groups. These became known by linguistic scholars as:

1. East Slav: Russian, Ukrainian and Belorussian, with about 200 million speakers today whose homelands are almost entirely in the former USSR.
2. South Slav: Serbo-Croat, Slovene, Macedonian and Bulgarian, the languages of Yugoslavia and Bulgaria.
3. West Slav: Polish, Czech, Slovak, Sorb and Kashubian.

A major preoccupation of the Western Slavs throughout history has been the struggle to resist cultural and economic domination by the Germans to the west and the Russians to the east. That struggle triggered the Second World War.

The suffering and loss of life at the hands of the Nazis in those war years was unspeakable, but language and culture survived. Post-war Poland and Czechoslovakia were reconstituted within new frontiers, albeit under the totalitarian rule of puppet Communist regimes subject to the unwelcome and oppressive 'protection' of the Soviet Red Army.

For decades all attempts to seek a freer and more democratic life, as in the 'Prague Spring' of 1968, were ruthlessly crushed by the Communists. Eventually the outlawed Polish trade union 'Solidarity' succeeded in setting in motion a process which in 1989 brought an end to Communist domination in Eastern Europe.

103

POLAND

The Polish state may be said to have started in 966 when Mieszko, Prince of the Polanians became a Christian. In 1385 Poland and Lithuania joined to challenge the might of the Teutonic Knights. By the mid 16th century a vast, multi-ethnic Polish-Lithuanian commonwealth stretched from the Baltic to the Black Sea.

The 17th and 18th centuries witnessed a decline in Polish influence and power to the extent that by 1795 the Russian, Prussian and Austro-Hungarian empires had completely partitioned Poland among them. The Polish state had ceased to exist.

The idea of Poland, its language, culture and Roman Catholic faith remained. A number of uprisings occurred in the following century, particularly against the Russians, but these were brutally suppressed. Yet in 1918, as the First World War came to an end, Poland regained its independence.

Tragedy again overtook Poland with the invasion in 1939 first by Germany and then by the Soviet Union, so heralding the Second World War. The war ended with Poland in ruins but reinstated under a Communist regime. In the process Poland lost 42% of its pre-war territory in the east but gained former German territory in the west. As a result Poland is now more homogeneous than formerly although there are Ukrainian, Kashubian, German, Belorussian and Czech minorities.

The formation of the free trade union 'Solidarity' in 1980 led eventually to the election in 1989 of the first non-Communist government in the Eastern bloc.

The white eagle on a red ground in the arms of Poland can be traced to the 13th century. The flag was adopted in 1918.

I

BOHEMIA

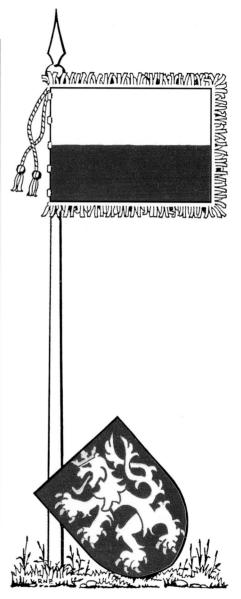

Around the 7th century the Czechs came to occupy territory to the south of the Erzgebirge and Sudetes Mountains and east of the Bavarian Forest, subsequently known as Bohemia-Moravia.

Borivoj, founder of the first Bohemian dynasty, converted to Christianity around AD 867. The kingdom grew in prestige under the suzerainty of the Holy Roman Empire. Its 'golden age' was the 14th century, when Bohemia ranked as one of the most cultured states in Europe.

The election of a Habsburg to the throne of Bohemia, however, started a process of Germanisation which accelerated with the defeat of the Czechs at the battle of White Mountain in 1620. After that, the Czech language was forbidden and the Czechs were denied the opportunity to acquire wealth or influence.

Oppression continued for two and a half centuries until, in the 19th century, activists strove to re-build interest in the Czech language and literature. Czechs were thereby stimulated to work towards raising themselves above the level of illiterate peasants to a point where they could achieve self-government.

After repeated rejection, this goal was finally achieved through the break-up of the Austro-Hungarian Empire in 1918. Bohemia, Moravia and Slovakia were amalgamated to form the new state of Czechoslovakia. From that date, Czech became an official language for the first time in three centuries.

The arms of Bohemia, a crowned silver lion on a red field, were granted in 1158 by the Holy Roman Emperor. The lion assumed its double tail a century later. The white and red bi-colour Czech flag dating from the late 19th century is still sometimes used.

MORAVIA

The fortunes of Moravia have been closely linked with those of Bohemia since time immemorial. Both areas have been inhabited by Czechs for some 1400 years.

Like Bohemia, Moravia fell under the domination of Austria in the 17th century. Although at times concessions were made to Czech autonomy, German became the dominant language until Czechoslovakia was formed in 1918. From that time the Czech language was given equal status with German.

Just before the Second World War, Czechoslovakia was invaded and dismembered by Hitler. Moravia and Bohemia were annexed to the Third Reich for the duration of the war. In 1946 Czechoslovakia was re-instated with a slightly reduced area, and much of the former German population was expelled.

The Soviet occupying forces installed a Communist regime. Moravia formed a constituent part of the new People's Republic of Czechoslovakia along with Bohemia and Slovakia. Premier Dubček's attempt to liberalise Czechoslovakia in 1968 was crushed by Soviet Red Army tanks and authoritarian rule reimposed.

With the liberalisation of the Soviet Union in the late 1980s and the popular demand for democracy sweeping through Eastern Europe, the Communist government gave up power in 1989 to make way for a long-awaited free, democratic and pluralist order.

The distinctive arms of Moravia, a checky eagle displayed, date from the 13th century. In 1920 the Czech bi-colour flag was modified by adding a triangle of blue to reflect the arms of Moravia and Slovakia, thereby displaying the Slav colours. It has been in official use by Czechoslovakia ever since.

D > A

SLOVAKIA

The area south of the Carpathian mountains, formerly inhabited by Celts, was eventually settled around the 7th century by the Slovaks, who spoke a language closely related to Czech.

As early as the 10th century Slovakia had become a land of the Hungarian crown. After the amalgamation of Austria and Hungary in 1526 the Habsburgs ruled Slovakia.

A Slovak renaissance and linguistic revival began late in the 18th century. After the Austro-Hungarian 'Ausgleich' or compromise, of 1867, however, the new Hungarian government policy of Magyarisation, suppressed everything Slovak.

With the break-up of the Habsburg Empire in 1918 Slovakia joined the new state of Czechoslovakia, within which the Slovak language gained the official status it had so long lacked. There was, however, resentment at Czech domination.

During the Second World War Slovakia was a nominally independent protectorate of Germany, but reunited with Bohemia and Moravia when Czechoslovakia was reconstituted in 1945. In 1969 a nominally autonomous Slovak Republic was created, now represented equally with the Czech lands in the Czechoslovak Federal Assembly.

Of the population of just over five million, nine-tenths are Slovak. The remainder are Hungarians, Czechs, Ukrainians, Germans, Russians and Poles.

The arms are the Patriarchal Cross of Slovakia. The flag, which is still used today, displays the pan-Slav colours adopted by the Slovaks in the 19th century as a symbol of their struggle for self-determination.

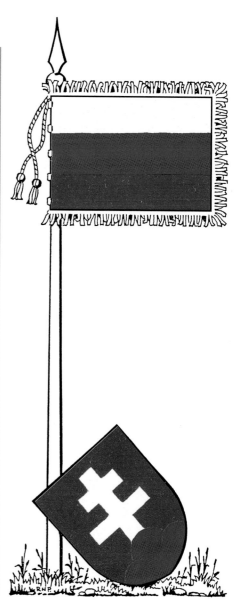

Af > I

The Byzantine Inheritance
SOUTH-EAST EUROPE

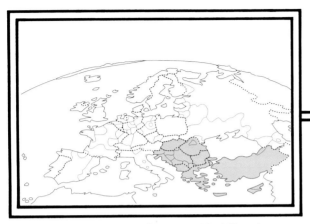

78 Turkey 79 Greece 80 Albania
81 Serbia 82 Slovenia 83 Croatia
84 Dalmatia 85 Bosnia
Hercegovina 86 Montenegro
87 Macedonia 88 Hungary
89 Bulgaria 90 Romania

In AD 330 the Roman Emperor Constantine, in an attempt to strengthen the Empire, founded a new eastern capital at Byzantium on the Bosphorus and renamed it Constantinople.

This eastern, or Byzantine, Empire based on Constantinople was to survive for almost 1000 years after Rome itself had fallen in 476. The Byzantine Empire became the heir to the heritage of Greece. It shone in art, learning and social practice, and it carried Christianity throughout its vast sphere of influence — in particular through the conversion of the various Slav peoples.

The 'orthodox' Christianity developed by the Byzantines was more mystical and liturgical than that of Rome and early use was made of vernacular languages in religious services. A lasting legacy is the alphabet, invented for the Slavs by the evangelist brothers Cyril and Methodius. The alphabet is still known as 'Cyrillic'.

During its Golden Age, Byzantium shielded the developing medieval Europe from the aggressive ambition of Islam, but as the pressure increased in the late 11th century, Emperor Alexius I reluctantly sought help from the west. So ensued the crusades, ostensibly holy in purpose, but in practice a series of plundering raids from which the Byzantine Empire itself suffered.

In the succeeding centuries, the Empire, which had hitherto embraced much of south-east Europe and the Middle East, contracted, as it was gradually overrun by the Ottoman Turks. The fortress city of Constantinople eventually fell to the Turks in 1453. Thus ended Constantine's splendid imperial creation.

TURKEY

In the 11th and 12th centuries nomadic Muslim Turkic people invaded eastern Anatolia. The Turkish leader Osman I established the Ottoman dynasty which thereafter waged a systematic campaign against the Byzantine Empire.

The Ottomans had overrun almost all the Byzantine territory of western Anatolia and south-eastern Europe by the 14th century. The Christian Balkan states became their vassals. The Ottomans finally conquered Constantinople in 1453.

At its height in the 16th century, Ottoman rule extended from Hungary to the Euphrates river and North Africa. After the reign of Suleiman II the Magnificent (1520–1566) the empire began to decline and by 1718 Austria had driven the Turks from Hungary.

The empire was finally dismembered, and both caliphate and sultanate abolished at the end of the First World War. The Turkish Republic was founded in 1923 by Mustafa Kemal Atatürk. He initiated a modernisation programme which included a drive for literacy, the adoption of Latin script in place of Arabic and the creation of modern secular institutions.

Only five per cent of modern Turkey is in Europe proper. The vast remainder occupies the former Byzantine lands of Anatolia (Asia Minor). Turkish is the mother tongue of 90% of the population. The main minorities are Kurds (7%), Arabs (1%) and also small groups of Greeks, Armenians and Jews. The recent human rights record of the Turkish state is appalling, particularly with regard to the Kurdish minority who seek independence.

The star and crescent flag and arms have been in use by the Turks since at least the 15th century.

I

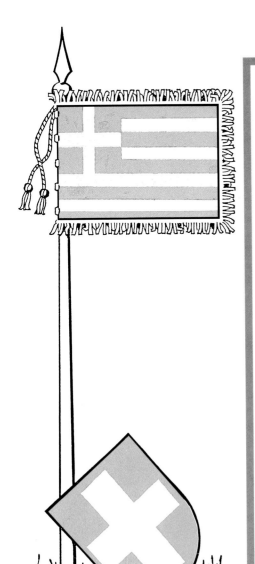

GREECE

The legacy of ancient Greece's achievements in the arts and sciences is fundamental to European civilisation. Even after its decline, the Romans were heavily influenced by the culture of Greece, which they conquered between 205 and 146 BC. The Greek language survived in the eastern half of the Roman Empire and grew in influence under the Byzantine Empire with the growth of Greek Orthodox Christianity.

By the 15th century, virtually all of Greece had fallen to the expanding and harsh Ottoman Empire. The Orthodox Church was, however, left intact and came to represent Greek nationalism.

After centuries of Turkish oppression, the Greeks rebelled in 1821 and sought to establish an independent kingdom. With the help of the western European powers and Russia, independence was achieved and recognised in 1830. The Bavarian Otto was placed on the throne in 1833.

Today the Hellenic Republic as a democracy is a full member of the European Community. The modern Greek language, closely related to ancient Greek, is spoken today on the Greek peninsula itself, most of the islands of the Aegean, the west coast of Anatolia (Turkey) and much of Cyprus. There are also Albanian, Bulgarian, Macedonian, Vlach and Turkish minorities in Greece. These, however, receive little cultural support from the Greek government.

The arms were adopted in 1863 when the Danish Prince William became King of the Greeks. A flag displaying a white cross on a blue field was used in the 1822 wars of liberation against the Turks. The striped version was adopted in 1833.

I

ALBANIA

A people apart, the Albanians have inhabited their remote mountainous heartland in the southern Balkans for a very long time. Although part of the Indo-European family, the Albanian language, with its archaic grammar, is not closely related to any others. It is thought to be descended from Illyrian.

Like other Balkan peoples, the Albanians were conquered by the Turks and incorporated into the Ottoman Empire in the 15th century. Whilst many northern Albanians remained Roman Catholics, most of the southern population became Muslim. Under Turkish rule Albania remained very backward.

An Albanian national awakening emerged in the 19th century and was focused in 1878 by the formation of the nationalist Prizren League. Its objects were to prevent the dismemberment of Albanian territory, to seek self-government and to establish Albanian as a national language. Intense literary activity followed but one difficulty was that Albanian had no standardised written form. A unified alphabet was not agreed until the 20th century.

Albania eventually achieved independence in 1913, a status it has enjoyed to the present day, apart from a period of Italian occupation between 1939 and 1944. Since then Albania's Communist regime has pursued an isolationist policy until the effect of the break-up of Communist regimes elsewhere has forced liberalisation. The secessionist demands of the Albanian majority in adjacent Serbian Kosovo may eventually lead to amalgamation of that territory with Albania.

The black double-headed eagle on a red field of the Albanian arms and flag were used by Albanian hero, Skanderbeg, who resisted the conquering Turks until his death in 1468.

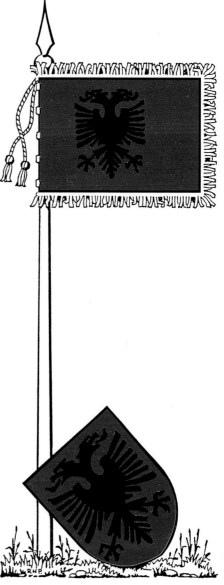

SERBIA

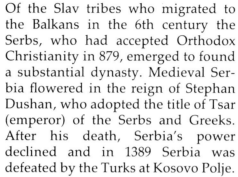

Of the Slav tribes who migrated to the Balkans in the 6th century the Serbs, who had accepted Orthodox Christianity in 879, emerged to found a substantial dynasty. Medieval Serbia flowered in the reign of Stephan Dushan, who adopted the title of Tsar (emperor) of the Serbs and Greeks. After his death, Serbia's power declined and in 1389 Serbia was defeated by the Turks at Kosovo Polje.

In 1459 Serbia was annexed to the Ottoman Empire, and for four centuries the Serbs lived under Turkish rule, although they preserved their speech and religion. Serbian uprisings commenced in the early 19th century. In 1829 Serbia became an autonomous Turkish principality, gaining full independence in 1878.

Serbia was proclaimed a kingdom in 1882 and in 1918 became the dominant power behind the new Kingdom of the Serbs, Croats and Slovenes, named Yugoslavia (South Slavia) in 1929. The reconstituted Communist Yugoslavia of 1946 reduced Serbia's size as Montenegro and Macedonia became separate republics.

Serbo-Croat is the major Yugoslav language, native to Serbia, Montenegro, Bosnia-Herzegovina and Croatia. The Serbs, however, use the Cyrillic alphabet. There are substantial Hungarian and Albanian populations in the nominally autonomous territories of Vojvodina and Kosovo respectively.

The Albanian majority in Kosovo resents Serbia's oppressive and intolerant dominance and has agitated for secession.

The arms of Serbia are based on those attributed to the Byzantine Empire. The four Cyrillic 'S-s' represent 'Only Unity Saves the Serbs'. The flag dates from 1835.

SLOVENIA

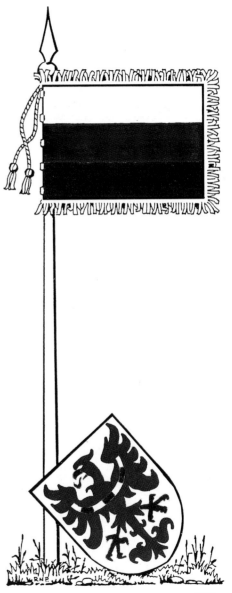

This southern Slav nation has occupied its region at the north-eastern end of the Adriatic since about the 6th century. In the 9th century the Slovenes were incorporated within the Frankish empire of Charlemagne. After its partition, Slovenia came under the rule of the German (Holy Roman) Empire.

German, and latterly Austrian, domination lasted for about 1000 years, with the Slovenes reduced to an under-class of illiterate serfs. The long Germanisation process was so persistent it is miraculous that the Slovene language has managed to survive.

Periodic Slovenian insurrections were ruthlessly crushed and it was not until 1750 that Marko Pohlin, an opponent of Germanisation, produced Slovenian school books. This was ridiculed at the time but it nevertheless stimulated others to work towards rehabilitation of the Slovene tongue.

Throughout the 19th century, despite setbacks, the Slovene national movement grew in strength. When the Austrian Empire collapsed in 1918 the Slovenes joined the new (Yugoslav) Kingdom of Serbs, Croats and Slovenes. There are Slovene minorities in Austria and Italy.

With its language and culture rehabilitated, Slovenia became the most prosperous and westernised component of Yugoslavia. In 1990, in the first multi-party elections since 1938, the Slovenes elected a non-Communist government which, despite armed Serbian opposition, achieved independence in 1991.

The arms shown are those of the Duchy of Carniola which coincides approximately with Slovenia. New arms of stars, mountains and the sea were adopted in 1991. The flag dates from 1848.

I

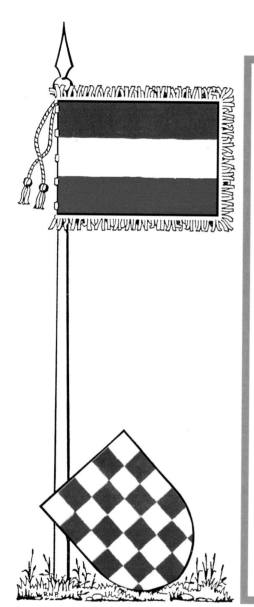

CROATIA

As part of the great 6th century migration of Slav tribes, the Croats settled in the former Roman provinces of Pannonia and Dalmatia. In the 7th century, in contrast to the Orthodox Serbs, the Croats adopted Roman Catholicism.

Croatia became a kingdom in the 10th century but was conquered by Ladislas I of Hungary in 1091. Croatia remained united to Hungary virtually continuously for eight centuries, even through a long period of Ottoman rule.

Although Croatia eventually enjoyed a measure of internal autonomy, the Croatian Diet broke off all ties with Hungary in 1918, proclaimed its independence, and entered into a union with the other Yugoslav lands of Serbia and Slovenia.

The Croat and Serbian languages are almost identical, apart from minor dialectical differences. They are, therefore, classed as a single Serbo-Croat language. Croat, however, is written using the Roman alphabet, reflecting Croatia's Roman Catholic and Western heritage.

During the Second World War, after Yugoslavia had been occupied by the Axis powers, an independent Fascist Croatian state was created in 1941. This succumbed to partisan resistance in 1945, whereupon Croatia rejoined Yugoslavia as one of the new constituent republics run on Communist principles. In 1990, however, the Croats voted for independence. In the face of armed conflict with Serbs, Croat independence was recognised in 1992.

The distinctive red and white checks on the Croatian arms are very ancient, and were first used by the old Croatian kings. The Croat tricolour flag dates from 1848.

DALMATIA

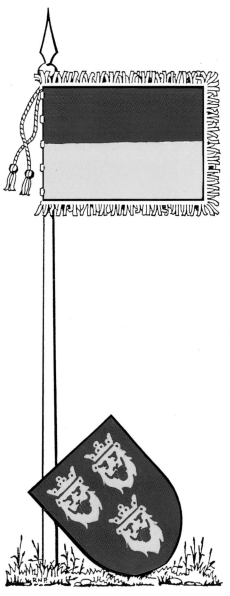

This narrow coastal region with its fringe of islands is separated from Bosnia-Herzegovina in the Dinaric Alps. It stretches 233 miles (375 km) along the Adriatic from the Kvarner Gulf to the narrows of Kotor. Its numerous bays, scenic beauty and mild climate make Dalmatia deservedly popular with tourists.

The first known inhabitants were Illyrians, an Indo-European people, who overran large parts of the Balkans around 1000 BC. Greeks also established colonies on a number of the islands from around the 4th century BC. A protracted conflict from 229 BC until 155 BC culminated in Roman occupation of the country.

After the fall of Rome, Dalmatia experienced some thirty changes of sovereignty. These included Byzantines, Greeks, Magyars, Tatars, Croatian and Serbian princes. Venetian rule lasted from 1420 to 1797. After this Dalmatia became an Austrian possession until 1918.

During the First World War, under the secret Treaty of London, Dalmatia was promised to Italy, but most was in fact incorporated into what was to become Yugoslavia in 1920. During the Second World War, Dalmatia was annexed by Italy, but in 1947 passed entirely to Yugoslavia as a region of the Croatian Republic, the regional capital being Split.

The Illyrian language became extinct around the 7th century, and likewise Dalmatian, a Romance language in the 19th century. The principal language in use today is Croatian, although Italian may still be heard.

The arms which display three lions' heads date from the Venetian period. The flag is traditional.

In ancient times this mountainous land was inhabited by Illyrian tribes, Slav settlement beginning in the 7th century. With the expansion of the Turks into the Balkans in the 15th century Bosnia fell under Turkish hegemony. Although there was little settlement by Turks, a proportion of the Slav population became Muslims.

Turkish rule lasted until a Balkan-wide revolt in 1875. Under the Treaty of Berlin which followed, the territory was mandated to the Austro-Hungarian Empire, whose administration was based on Sarajevo under a governor. Eventually in 1908 Bosnia and Hercegovina were annexed by Aus-tria-Hungary and granted a very limited and ineffectual form of autonomy.

Political confusion and revolutionary ferment led to the assassination of the Austrian Archduke Franz Ferdinand in June 1914, so setting in train the First World War.

After the war, Bosnia and Hercegovina was incorporated into Yugoslavia. In 1991, on declaration of independence, this most ethnically diverse of the Yugoslav republics became the subject of territorial dispute between Serbs, Croats and Muslims, who account for 31%, 17% and 45% respectively of the population.

The arms are those used by the Austrians after freedom from Turkish rule. The traditional flag shown is based on the pan-Slav colours, used also by Yugoslavia. The post-war official flag of Bosnia-Hercegovina has been red with the traditional flag, charged with a partisan star, in canton.

MONTENEGRO

Named the 'Black Mountain' by the Venetians, the rugged independent Slav province of Zeta was absorbed into the Serbian empire in the 12th century. It regained its independence in 1389 following defeat of the Serbs by the Turks.

By repulsing intermittent Turkish attacks, this precarious independence was tenaciously maintained through the centuries until 1918. Then once again Montenegro was somewhat unwillingly absorbed into Serbia and the newly created Yugoslav monarchy of the Serbs, Croats and Slovenes.

During the Second World War, Montenegran partisans vigorously resisted the Italian occupation. After the war, Montenegro formed one of the six nominally autonomous republics of a reconstituted Yugoslavia run on Communist principles.

The mother-tongue of most Montenegrans is Serbian, although there is an Albanian minority.

In 1992, as the four non-Serb republics seceded from Yugoslavia, Montenegro opted to remain part of the Yugoslav federation. It is probable, therefore, that Montenegro will form an autonomous region of a new 'Greater Serbia'.

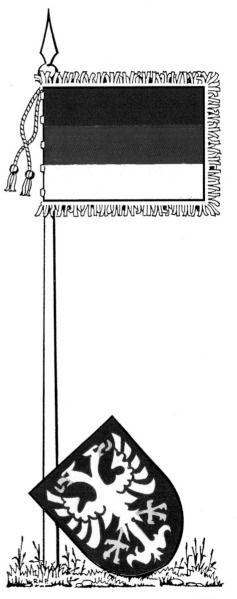

The arms originate with the medieval province of Zeta. The tricolour flag illustrated dates from around 1880, although since 1946, in common with other Yugoslav republics, the official version was with a red partisan star, representing the victory of Communism.

Af

MACEDONIA

The immense power of Alexander the Great, king of Macedonia, was legendary in ancient times. By the 4th century Macedonia had become a Roman province and by the 7th century it had become a Slav land. It has remained so ever since.

As the Ottoman Empire in the Balkans was steadily pushed back in the 19th century, Macedonia, together with Albania, was among the last to be free of Turkish rule. As these events unfolded, a dispute arose among Serbia, Greece and Bulgaria over possession of Macedonia.

Eventually, after a brief war in 1913, Macedonia was divided among the three, the largest part going to Serbia. Additional territory was gained from Bulgaria in 1919.

A national council was formed during the Second World War, since when Macedonia became recognised as a separate constituent republic of Yugoslavia. The republic of today comprises the western half of the historic region of Macedonia. The capital is Skopje.

Macedonian is a south Slavic language, closely related to Bulgarian and written in the Cyrillic alphabet. It is spoken by two thirds of the population and has been the official language of Macedonia since the establishment of the republic. It is also spoken in adjacent areas of Greece and Bulgaria. There are Albanian, Turkish and Serbian enclaves. Macedonian independence was declared in 1991.

The ancient arms are closely related to those of Bulgaria and the traditional flag shown is the banner of the arms. The official flag is red with a partisan star in canton.

HUNGARY

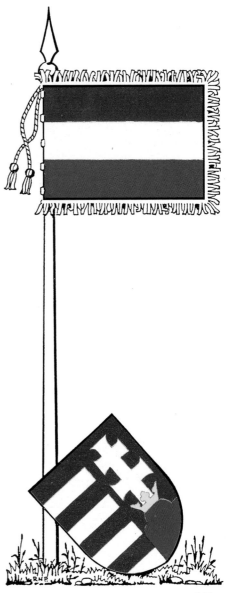

The Hungarians, or Magyars as they call themselves, are a (non Indo-European) Ugric people who stormed across Eastern Europe and began settling in the Danubian plain around the year 900. They menaced Western Europe until their defeat by Emperor Otto I in 955.

On Christmas Day 1000, (Saint) Stephen became Hungary's first Christian king. His crown is kept and cherished to this day. The fortunes of the Hungarian state have fluctuated considerably over the centuries, as have its boundaries. Hungary has been occupied or ruled in whole or in part by the Mongols of Genghis Khan, the kings of Naples, Bohemia, Bavaria, the Ottoman Turks and the Austrian Habsburgs.

The Hungarian frontier formerly embraced a considerable non-Hungarian population. It now more closely approximates to the Hungarian ethnic territory, although there are substantial Hungarian communities in Romania, Slovakia and Serbia. There is also a sizeable German minority in Hungary.

Since the late 1940s Hungary came under the Soviet sphere of influence and a Communist form of government was imposed. A popular uprising against the Communists in 1956 was crushed by the Red Army. In 1989, however, democratic pluralism was readopted by the Hungarians.

The arms of Hungary are ancient — eight horizontal red and silver bars (known since 1202) — and modern — a double cross on three green mounds. After decades of suppression by the Communist regime, the ancient arms were officially reinstated in 1989. The flag takes its colours from the coat of arms.

I

BULGARIA

The original Bulgars were a Turkic tribe from central Asia who crossed the Danube from the north in the 7th century. They subjugated the more numerous local Slav population, whose language they adopted. Conversion to Orthodox Christianity by their king, Boris I in 864, facilitated the growth of the First and Second Bulgarian Empires (893–927 and 1185–1396).

For five centuries thereafter, Bulgaria fell under Ottoman rule. It was not until the 1870s that a movement known as the 'National Revival' emerged to focus Bulgarian identity. Bulgaria gained full internationally recognised independence as a monarchy in 1908.

In the Second World War Bulgaria sided with the Germans. With the invasion of the Soviet Red Army in 1944 the monarchy was abolished and a centrally controlled Communist People's Republic formed. This repressive style of government continued until 1989 when the Communist leadership resigned. Democratic elections followed in 1990.

Ethnically, Bulgarians make up about 85% of the population. There are sizeable Turkish, Macedonian, Greek and Gypsy minorities. Macedonians were not recognised by the Communist authorities as distinct from Bulgarians. Until 1990 Turks in particular, who resisted a systematic Bulgarianisation process, were severely harassed.

Most Bulgarians who profess a religion are Orthodox.

The national flag, which is a variant of the pan-Slav flag, was adopted in 1878. The golden lion on a red (or purple) field has been the arms of the Bulgarian czar since the 14th century.

ROMANIA

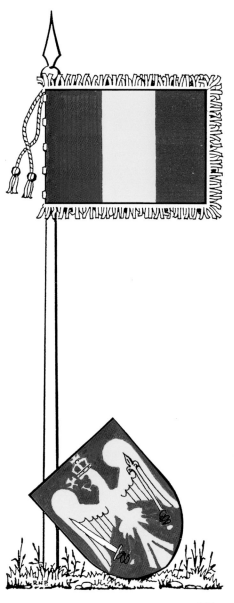

The Romanians are a Latin people, of mainly Orthodox faith, surrounded by Slavs and Magyars. Like other eastern Europeans they rose against Turkish rule in the mid 19th century when the state of Romania was created. By the 1920s Romania was one of the most advanced of the East European countries.

After the Second World War, a Communist regime was established which was in time to evolve into the most oppressive in all Europe. The notorious 24-year dictatorship of Nicolae Ceaucescu ruined the economy and the living standards of the people, while any form of dissent was ruthlessly suppressed by the hated secret police — the Securitate.

After the liberalisation of the other 'Eastern bloc' countries during 1989, the regime finally overstepped the hard-pressed population's tolerance. In December of that year large numbers of unarmed demonstrators were massacred in the town of Timisoara. Nationwide, the people rose against the dictator and after a week of violent fighting the regime was overthrown. The Romanian people's nightmare was over.

Although Romanians predominate, there is a large Hungarian minority and smaller German and Turkish communities. To the north of Romania lies the Soviet Republic of Moldavia whose majority population also speak a form of Romanian. As life in Romania returns to normal, it is likely that pressure will increase for amalgamation of Moldavia and Romania.

The traditional arms of Romania (suppressed by the Communists) displaying an eagle with a cross in its beak are based on the ancient arms of the important province of Wallachia. The tricolour flag appeared in the 19th century.

Soviet Transformation
THE FORMER USSR IN EUROPE

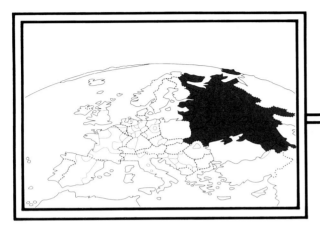

91 Russia   92 Ukraine
93 Belarus   94 East Prussia
95 Lithuania   96 Latvia
97 Estonia   98 Georgia
99 Armenia   100 Azerbaijan

The Great War was a disaster for the old Russian Empire and brought about its collapse. After a brief period of provisional government under Kerensky, Lenin and his (Communist) Bolsheviks seized power in the October Revolution of 1917.

Freed from central authority, the various nationalities of the old empire set about establishing autonomous or independent states. After a protracted and bloody civil war, however, the Bolsheviks succeeded in imposing their authority over most of the former Russian Empire and in 1922 drew the new states together to form the Union of Soviet Socialist Republics (USSR).

The rule of Joseph Stalin, who succeeded Lenin, was notorious for its cynical brutality and genocide. His regime did, however, transform the USSR into a world industrial power and played a major part in the military defeat of Nazi Germany.

Stalin's death in 1953 brought some softening of the most oppressive features of the Soviet regime. It was not until the accession to power of Mikhail Gorbachev in 1985 that a process of fundamental change was set in motion which would liberalise not only the USSR itself, but all Eastern Europe.

The power struggle between those who favoured a centralised authoritarian state, and advocates of democracy and self-determination for the diverse Soviet nationalities climaxed in a bungled coup by Communist hard-liners who had sought to reverse reforms. The authority of the Communist Party was broken. The ensuing secession of the republics led to the collapse of the USSR and the formation of a new 'Commonwealth of Independent States' (CIS).

RUSSIA

When the Mongols of the Golden Horde occupied the lands of the eastern Slavs in the 13th and 14th centuries, Christian Slav principalities such as Novgorod and Muscovy continued to follow a semi-autonomous existence, by acting as agents to the Mongols.

As the Golden Horde experienced internal dissent in the mid 14th century, Muscovy (Moscow) in particular became increasingly successful in exploiting this weakness. Territorial expansion and diplomatic success were consolidated by Ivan III (1462–1505). His son Ivan IV the Terrible became first Tsar of Russia in 1547.

From 1613 the Romanov dynasty was established. It was to endure until the 1917 Revolution. By that time a vast multi-ethnic Russian Empire stretched from the Baltic to the Pacific, embracing about one sixth of the global land surface.

This empire was inherited by the USSR. Although recognition was given to ethnic and linguistic diversity, the Russians were to remain dominant, with Russian actively promoted as the 'common' Soviet language, and the Russian Republic (RSFSR) occupying three-quarters of the total area of the USSR.

With the collapse of the USSR in 1991, the newly independent Russia led the formation of the CIS.

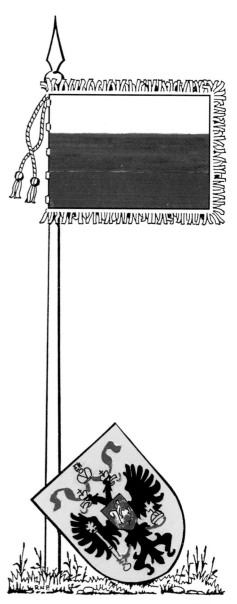

The beautiful arms shown are those of the Tsars. Three flags were commonly used in pre-revolutionary Russia: a white, blue, red tricolour, a white, orange, black tricolour and the ensign of a blue saltire on white. After over seventy years of suppression all three types reappeared in 1989 in popular demonstrations, the version shown being adopted officially in 1991.

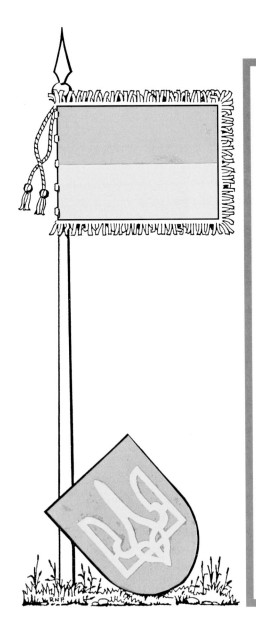

UKRAINE

This 'granary of Europe' forming the Ukrainian ethnic territory is larger in area than any other state in Europe, except Russia.

The first Ukrainian state was founded around Kyiv in the 9th century by Swedish Viking adventurers. By the 11th and 12th centuries the powerful Slavic kingdom of Rus had emerged. Subsequently the western Ukraine became part of the vast Grand Duchy of Lithuania, but by the end of the 17th century autonomy succumbed to annexation by the Russian and the Austro-Hungarian Empires.

The dream of national freedom continued to live and eventually bore fruit with the Revolution of 1917 and the collapse of Austria-Hungary in 1918.

A new Ukrainian republic was formed in 1918, but for three years was fought over by the Nationalist Army, the Red Army, the White Army and the Poles. Peace came at the end of 1922 when Ukraine became one of the four founding members of the USSR. In the next two decades millions of Ukrainians were to die, through famine deliberately organised by Stalin, and subsequently during the Second World War.

Traditionally the western Ukrainians are Uniates (Catholics) as distinct from the Orthodox adherents in the east. The Ukrainian language is spoken today by about 45 million people, of whom 5–6 million live in adjacent territory.

Ukrainian independence was achieved in 1991.

The golden trident of St. Volodyumyr on a sky-blue shield has served as a Ukrainian emblem since ancient times and was re-adopted in 1918. The flag was adopted in 1848 by the Supreme Ruthenian Council in Lviv. After nearly 70 years suppression, it was officially re-adopted in 1991.

BELARUS

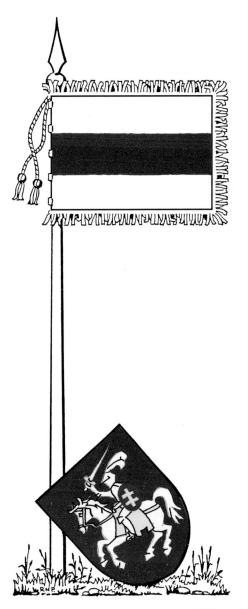

The White Russians, or Belorussians, are descendants of East Slavic tribes who settled the area between the 6th and 8th centuries. Subjugated in turn by Lithuania, Poland, then in the 18th century by Russia, Belorussia finally achieved independence towards the end of the First World War.

This regime was eventually overthrown by the Bolsheviks prior to incorporation in 1922 as one of the four founding members of the USSR. Between 1921 and 1939 western Belorussia again temporarily fell under Polish rule.

In the course of the Second World War, or the 'Great Patriotic War' as it was termed in the Soviet Union, Belorussia bore the brunt of the German invasion. Human loss and suffering reached unspeakable proportions and over 400 villages were obliterated. This experience has left an indelible mark on the collective psyche of the Belorussians.

Today Belarus as it is now called, which includes former Polish territory, has largely made good the immense physical war damage. The majority of those who adhere to a church are Orthodox Christians. Some 80% of the population speak Belorussian, the official language.

Belarus became independent in 1991.

The arms, a mounted knight with a gold passion cross on his blue buckler, originated in the period of Lithuanian ascendency. On achieving independence, Belorussia briefly had a plain white flag, replaced in 1917 by the white-red-white flag shown, until superseded, as with other republics of the USSR, by a series of Communist flags. In 1989 however, the white-red-white flag re-emerged as a symbol of Belorussian independence, being adopted officially in 1991.

I

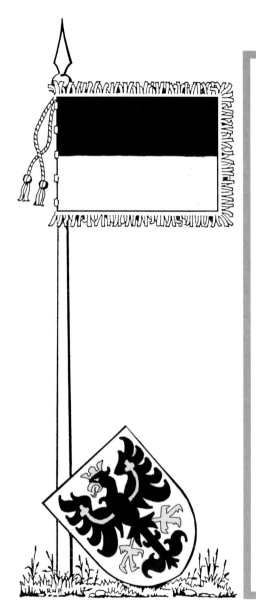

EAST PRUSSIA

The militant Teutonic Order of Knights had originally been formed at the end of the 12th century for conquest of the Holy Land. In 1229 a contingent was sent to subdue and baptise the pagan (Baltic) Prussians in the southern Baltic coast lands.

The lands they conquered were controlled by great castles and towns like Königsberg (since 1945, Kaliningrad). East Prussia came under Brandenburg hegemony in the 17th century to form the eastern part of the Prussian empire which eventually dominated Germany.

Although German territory since the Middle Ages, East Prussia was eliminated at the end of the Second World War. The bulk of the population was killed or expelled with considerable further suffering and loss of life. With its strategic position on the Baltic Sea, northern East Prussia was absorbed by the Russian SFSR. Poland occupied the remainder, together with the rest of eastern Germany as far as the Oder and Western Neisse rivers.

The collapse of the USSR leaves the future of East Prussia unclear. Autonomy within Russia or independence in association with either the other Baltic lands, Poland or even Germany are future possibilities.

The black Prussian eagle is well known as the symbol of Imperial Germany. Neither the eagle nor the dramatically simple black and white flag are to be seen today on East Prussian territory. They are, however, used by exiles who dream of returning to their homeland.

D > Af or [> I]

LITHUANIA

Unlike the other Baltic lands (Latvia and Estonia), Lithuania rose to become a great power. By the 15th century her sphere of influence extended from the Baltic to the Black Sea, embracing much of present-day White Russia and Ukraine.

The period of greatness was followed by decline and dismemberment and in 1795 Lithuania was absorbed by the Russian Empire. Russian rule was oppressive but the Lithuanian national spirit remained in the hearts of the people and following the 1905 revolution, a Lithuanian Congress called for home rule.

This came in February 1918 and the Soviet Union recognised Lithuanian sovereignty in the peace treaty of 1920. This independence was ended by the Soviet invasion of 1940 and subsequent incorporation within the Soviet Union.

As demands for greater self-determination swept through the republics of the USSR in the late 1980s, Lithuania opened up a dialogue with Moscow with a view to seeking greater autonomy. In building up a broad and well-organised consensus for reform, Lithuania became the leader of the Baltic independence movement.

In 1990 Lithuania declared her independence. The USSR responded by imposing an economic blocade backed by increased military presence. A period of tense uncertainty followed, but international recognition of Lithuania's independence was achieved in 1991.

The arms date from medieval times. The flag is that used by the independent republic between World Wars I and II, and after nearly half a century of suppression, was officially re-adopted in 1989 as a result of popular pressure.

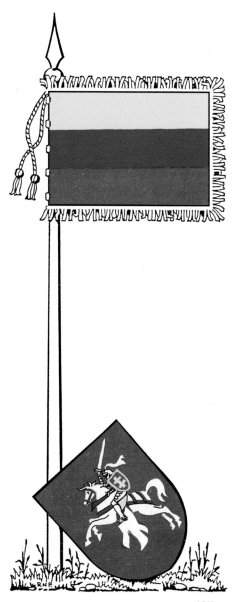

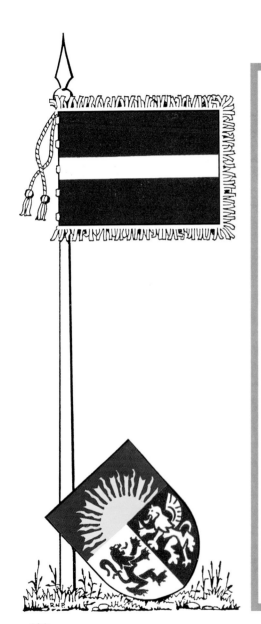

LATVIA

Latvians and Lithuanians are descended from the same ancestral stock. Their languages are the only survivors of the archaic Baltic family, quite distinct from the Germanic and Slavonic languages. Conquered in the 13th century by the Teutonic Knights under the guise of a crusade, the Latvians were reduced to the status of serfs in their own land. Rule over Latvia changed hands through the years between Germans, Poles, Swedes and Russians.

A vigorous renaissance of Latvian culture in the 19th century, against official hostility, together with increasing education and economic activity, led eventually to demands for autonomy.

The collapse of both German and Russian Empires at the end of World War I provided the opportunity to create the independent republic of Latvia in 1918. The new republic flourished but in 1940 the Red Army invaded Latvia ending its independence and, as with the other Baltic states, illegally incorporating it into the USSR.

Until the mid 1950s, many Latvians suffered deportation, imprisonment, torture and murder. The language furthermore, has been under pressure from large-scale Russian immigration.

In active cooperation with the other Baltic republics, the Latvians won political independence which was internationally recognised in 1991.

The arms represent the main provinces together with the military cockade. The flag dates from the 13th century. Both were used during the period of independence. They were officially re-adopted in 1989 with much emotion, after nearly 50 years of suppression.

ESTONIA

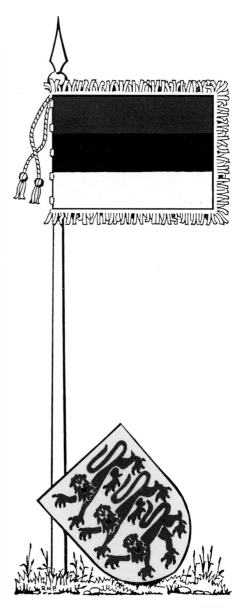

The Estonians, linguistically related to the Finns, lost their independence in 1227 through invasion by the German Teutonic Knights and the Danes. Centuries of foreign domination followed and by the 18th century Estonia was incorporated into the Russian Empire. Despite two further centuries of oppression, Estonian culture and national identity survived.

The collapse of the Tsarist Russian Empire during the First World War gave the Estonians the opportunity to declare national independence in 1918. A war of liberation was subsequently fought against the Bolsheviks and the Germans, and concluded successfully in the 1920 Peace of Tartu, in which the new Soviet Union 'voluntarily and for ever' renounced all rights over Estonia.

Between the wars, the newly independent Republic of Estonia achieved an outstanding expansion of its economic, social and cultural life. In 1940, however, under the secret terms of the notorious Nazi-Soviet pact, Soviet forces invaded Estonia, ending its independence and beginning a new period of oppression and deportation.

As a Soviet republic, Estonians faced the threat of becoming a minority in their own country because of a deliberate programme of Russification and of immigration from other parts of the USSR. However, after 'perestroika' swept through the USSR, Estonia won her independence in 1990/1.

The 1248 arms were those of Danish Revel (Tallinn). The flag originally designed by students in 1881, and was adopted as national flag in 1918. On incorporation within the USSR its use was forbidden, until readopted by popular demand in 1989.

GEORGIA

Georgia, or K'artveli, has been an independent kingdom since the days of Herodotus and had established an organised Christian Church by the 4th century. The pre Indo-European Georgian language, thought by some linguists to be remotely related to Basque, has had its own alphabet since AD 450.

In 1801 Georgia became a protectorate, and later a province of the Russian Empire. In 1917 the country became an independent republic recognised by the League of Nations, but by 1922 was absorbed into the USSR as the Georgian Soviet Socialist Republic, capital Tbilisi.

Two-thirds of the population of the GSSR are Georgians. Minorities include Armenians (10%), Russians and Azeris. Adzhars, Abkhazians and Ossetins in Georgia seek their own autonomous states. There are also Georgians in parts of Azerbaijan and some 200,000 in north-east Turkey.

In 1989 a peaceful all-night vigil in Tbilisi, of unarmed Georgian nationalists supporting a hunger strike, was attacked by Soviet troops, killing 20, mainly women. From that time demands for Georgian democracy and independence have accelerated without further interference from Moscow. The achievement of independence in 1991 was marred by armed internecine conflict.

The arms, which make punning reference to St. George, were used in Georgia by the Tsarist regime and later by the Georgian administration during its brief period of independence. The flag, of wine-red with bars of black (earth) and white (sky) was that used by the independent government. Suppressed by the Soviet authorities for 68 years, it re-emerged dramatically in 1989 as a national symbol in independence demonstrations.

ARMENIA

The Armenians are an ancient Indo–European people who have lived in the Caucasus since pre-historic times. The Armenian state, which in the past also covered much of what is now eastern Turkey, was founded in 624 BC. In AD 301 their ruler Tiridates was the first to declare Christianity a state religion.

The 4th and 5th centuries saw a level of scholarship and cultural achievement undreamt of in Western Europe. By the 16th century, however, Armenia fell into a long and disastrous decline under the harsh rule of the Turks and Persians. By 1828 eastern Armenia was annexed by the Russian Empire.

National revival began in the 19th century but perhaps the worst disaster occurred in the early 20th century when some two million Armenians were systematically exterminated by the Turkish authorities. An independent Armenian republic was created in 1918 which in 1922 became a member republic of the Soviet Union. Independence was re-established in 1991.

At the beginning of the 20th century the Armenian language was on the verge of extinction. Today it is a vibrant national language. The several linguistic minorities in Armenia include Georgians, Azeris and Kurds. There are also Armenian communities outside the republic, such as the Nagorno-Karabakh enclave in Azerbaijan, where serious ethnic and religious conflict has led to demands for its return to Armenia.

The lion in the arms of Armenia is an ancient symbol, said to have been derived from the lion of Judah. The flag is that used by the independent republic between 1918 and 1920. This flag was forbidden by the Soviet authorities, but in 1988 it re-emerged as a symbol of Armenian nationalism. It was officially re-adopted in 1991.

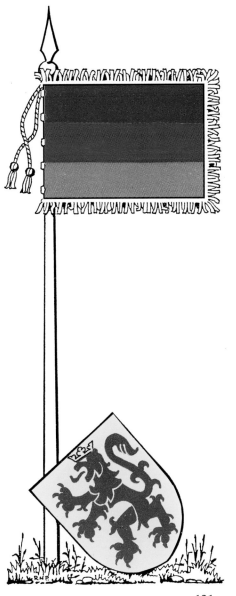

AZERBAIJAN

Known in antiquity as 'Land of Fire', due to the spontaneous combustion of escaping natural gas, Azerbaijan is today a substantial oil producer. The capital, Baku, is the fifth largest city of the former USSR.

Turkic in speech but originally of Caucasian stock, the people of Azerbaijan came under Muslim influence in the 7th century. They were incorporated into the Safavid Iranian empire in the 16th century and annexed in part by Russia in the early 19th century.

The former Russian (northern) territory became independent in 1918 but was overrun by the Red Army in 1920. This area formed the Azerbaijan SSR. About half the 10 million Azeri people live there, forming about 80% of the republic's population. Some four million live in the adjoining Iranian province of Azerbaijan. Smaller groups live in neighbouring republics.

Since 1988 Azerbaijan has been the scene of much violent ethnic upheaval, particularly between the majority (Muslim) Azeris and minority (Christian) Armenians. By 1990 demands for Azeri independence encouraged activists to challenge the Soviet authorities by tearing down the border fence separating the Soviet Azeris from their kin in Iranian Azerbaijan. Although subsequently restrained by Soviet forces, the reunification of Azerbaijan, perhaps in some form of association with Turkey, seems to be a future possibility.

The arms echo the colours of the flag which is charged with the traditional Muslim star and crescent. Arms and flag are as used during the brief period of independence. They came back into popular use in 1989 and were subsequently offically re-adopted.

Variations on a Theme

EASTERN EUROPEAN MINORITIES

The principal nations in the European part of the former USSR have already been described — namely the three dominant Slav nations of Russia, Ukraine and Belorus, East Prussia, the three Baltic nations and the Georgians, Armenians and Azeris in the Transcaucasus. The Moldavians, who won independence in 1991, are also mentioned in connection with Romania, with which country their long-term future is likely to lie.

Many other minorities also exist in the Soviet Union, including dispersed communities of Germans, Jews and Gypsies. The Transcaucasian area in particular is a linguistic treasure house. Within this rich mosaic some 6.6 million speak about 30 languages belonging to three distinct branches of the archaic, pre-Indo-European Caucasian family. Of these Georgian, with its venerable literature, is the most widely spoken. All others, except Chechen and Avar have fewer than half a million speakers. Some indeed are spoken only in single remote valleys.

The Indo-Iranian branch of the Indo-European languages are represented by the Ossetins, Tats, Talysh and Kurds. Besides widely spoken Azeri, other languages of the Altalc family are spoken by the (Turkic) Kumyk, Nogay, Tatar, Karachay, Balkar, Chuvash, Gaganz, and the (Mongol) Kalmyk peoples. Most Altalc people are Muslim but the Chuvash and Gaganz are Christian.

In northerly areas the minority peoples are mostly of Finnic speech. A large Karelian population lives adjacent to the Finnish border in what was formerly, and could again become, Finnish territory, and a small group of Samis have links with their kin in Scandinavia. An extensive area west of the Urals has long been settled by related Komi and Udmurt people and the central Volga area is home for Mordvin and Mari communities. In the Arctic littoral nomadic and sparsely distributed Samoyed people manage to find a living.

DISPERSED MINORITIES

Europe's national groups are each generally located in their defined, continuous and geographically circumscribed territories although there is often a measure of overlap or 'fuzziness' in border areas. In some cases substantial enclaves exist totally surrounded by people of a different ethnic group; examples are the Armenian enclave of Nagorno-Karabakh in Azerbaijan, and the large Hungarian enclave in Romania.

There are, however, national groups with a much more dispersed settlement pattern. While the Germans have a well defined 'Fatherland', scattered settlements of Germans have existed for centuries in eastern Europe, including over a million still in the USSR despite massive deportations in 1945/6.

Another people of widely dispersed, mainly urban, settlement, but for many centuries with no home territory, are the Jews, whose religion is the precursor of both Christianity and Islam. Despite these credentials, the Jews have suffered much persecution. During the Second World War six million were killed in the Nazi death camps.

Migration has created many scattered communities of various endogenous European peoples including Armenians and Italians, but since the end of the Second World War there has emerged a new phenomenon of large-scale immigration by a wide variety of exogenous peoples from the former European overseas colonies.

133

This diverse infusion has greatly enriched European culture, cuisine and outlook but inevitably there have been conflicts. Such conflicts are not new but their ultimate resolution lies in the fostering of understanding and mutual respect between peoples of all cultures and creeds.

NOMADIC PEOPLES

While most Europeans identify with their own defined ethnic territories, some have a less precise relationship with territory and state. This is particularly so of peoples whose cultures are based on a nomadic way of life.

Long ago nomadic life was the norm, but as agriculture developed, life in general became more territorially fixed. One people who still carry on the nomadic tradition, in part at least, are the Sami (or Lapps) whose economy has long been based on reindeer herding.

The 30,000 Sami, whose language is closely related to Finnish, inhabit a vast tract of land (Sapmi) stretching from northern Norway, through Sweden and Finland to the Kola peninsula in Arctic Russia. The rich culture and social structure of the Sami has been under threat for many years but is now being actively protected by the Norwegian government in particular.

Another people of migratory tradition are the Gypsies or Rom. They originated in northern India, reaching south-eastern and western Europe by the 14th and 15th centuries respectively. The estimated 2 to 3 million Gypsies are to be found throughout Europe and indeed world-wide.

During the Second World War the Nazis exterminated 400,000 Gypsies. Although denigrated and harrassed for centuries, there are strict social controls within Gypsy society. Many speak Romany, a language closely related to the Indo-European languages of northern India. Romany has a rich oral tradition but no real literature.

Nomadic Gypsies tend to migrate seasonally, often ignoring national boundaries. Many states seek to enforce settlement of Gypsies and migration is less prevalent than formerly.

THE DIVISION OF CYPRUS

Throughout history as new states have emerged, so have old states been absorbed or in some cases dismembered; Poland was a classic historical example. Current evidence suggests that Cyprus may disappear as a sovereign state.

Greek culture and language were introduced in ancient times to this eastern Mediterranean island. Christianity reached Cyprus as early as AD 45. Cyprus was part of the (Greek) Byzantine Empire for many centuries until the Middle Ages when Genoese and Venetian merchants gained increasing control.

Ottoman Turks conquered the island in 1573. At first their rule was liberal, but in later centuries became harsh. This provoked uprisings in the 18th and 19th centuries. In 1878, the British assumed control, formally annexing Cyprus in 1915.

A Greek Cypriot movement for *enosis* (union) with Greece emerged and grew in strength and violence after the Second World War, while the minority Muslim Turkish population agitated for partition. An independent republic was formed in 1960.

The Cypriot National Guard under Greek officers staged a coup in 1974. In response Turkey invaded and set up a separate Turkish state in the northern third of the island. Although not recognised internationally, there has been substantial resettlement of Greeks and Turks to their respective zones.

Despite geographical unity, cultural division has made a politically unified Cyprus difficult to sustain. Incorporation of the separate zones into Greece and Turkey respectively may yet occur despite international pressure for reconciliation.

ALTERNATIVE DEVELOPMENTS

Unlike the individual constitutionally similar states of the United States of America, the 100 European nations described in this book represent a very wide spectrum of status, background and potential. Rather than seek total uniformity of treatment, the selection has set out instead to illustrate the variety of ways in which national identity can develop political form.

The main thrust of the text is designed to show how yesterday's stateless nations are, each in their own way, pursuing their quest for greater self-determination, whether as wholly independent states or autonomous territories under the hegemony of a larger state. Examples of renascent nations include Scotland, Brittany, Slovenia, Latvia . . .

Also addressed is the inevitable corollary of this process, the future reduced role of the formerly dominant states such as England, France, Serbia, Russia, whose tutelage over the above peoples is no longer tenable.

In federal states like Germany, the self-government of individual and equal states is, as in the USA, an integral and essential feature of the body politic. Spain, whilst not federal, has, since the demise of Franco, created a regime in which variable degrees of self-government have been devolved to the non-Castilian peoples. Following the demise of the USSR, the Commonwealth of Independent States, a hybrid confederal structure, is evolving which may eventually merge with the European Community.

A further category embraces communities currently well rooted in the state in which they are located but who nevertheless feel themselves sufficiently distinct to foster overtly their local identity. Examples are Cornwall, Schaumberg-Lippe and Dalmatia. There are many others not covered by the main body of the text.

There are clearly alternatives to the '100 Nations' as set out here. The options are particularly interesting in the newly united Germany in which the five reconstituted eastern *Länder* added to the established ten in the west make fifteen (plus Berlin). This arrangement has never been regarded as permanent and further reorganisation has been mooted. From among the almost infinite permutations, the main text describes twenty units which exhibit some form of national or local identity and which can be considered as the building blocks of a reorganised federal structure. One fascinating possibility (explored in Figure 4) is a

FIG. 4 – GERMAN ALTERNATIVES

Today's *Länder*	The 20 units	The Big Six
Schleswig Holstein	Schleswig Holstein	Lower Saxony
Hamburg	Hamburg	
Bremen	Bremen	
Lower Saxony	Hanover	
	Brunswick-Lüneburg	
	Oldenburg	
	Schaumberg-Lippe	
N. Rhine Westphalia	Westphalia	
Rhineland Palatinate	Rhineland	Franconia
	Palatinate	
Hesse	Hesse	
Saarland	Saarland	
Baden Wurttemberg	Swabia	Swabia
Bavaria	Bavaria	Bavaria
Berlin*	Berlin	Marchlands
Mecklenburg Vorpommern	Mecklenburg Pomerania	
Brandenburg	Brandenburg	
Thuringia	Thuringia	Sax Thuringia
Saxony	Saxony	
Saxony Anhalt		

* Berlin is not a *Land*

reduction in the number of *Länder* to as few as six, corresponding simultaneously with Germany's main dialect areas and with the great tribal duchies of the 10th century.

Of the Germanic groups, the scattered coastal and island peoples of north Friesland in Schleswig-Holstein no longer have sufficient cohesion for viable political autonomy. They do, however, have a renewed sense of common bond and identity to promote their cultural, linguistic and economic interests through the international Frisian Council.

Throughout Europe, besides the well-defined nations, there exist provinces of long standing historical pedigree. Many have a strong sense of local identity and in some like Andalusia in Spain, Lombardy in Italy, and Ossetia in the former USSR, this finds active political expression.

It may well be that in the new Europe, the sense of local identity in some of these communities may in time become sufficiently developed to evolve into real autonomy or independence. Indeed as the world grows in complexity, this trend towards greater democratic local responsibility for local affairs is likely to grow.

Towards the New Europe

Europe's nations and ethnic minorities each have their own histories and their own destinies. Their quest for political, economic and cultural self-determination is inextricably bound up with Europe's progress towards unification. The hundred nations, as distinct from the existing nation states, are what can be understood as the 'organic' expression of Europe's peoples. They are the building blocks for the development of what Mikhail Gorbachev has described as the 'Common European Home'.

These naturally occurring 'organic' nations, with their deeply rooted ethnic and historical credentials, are not to be confused with the artificial economic 'regions' designated by planners and administrators to give spurious substance to the concept of a 'Europe of Regions' — a concept which could, if insensitively applied, actually undermine the healthy development of identity and self-confidence.

In the post-war years the existence of two ideologically opposed blocs frustrated the evolution of the pan-European idea and the prospect of self-determination for suppressed peoples. The brake came off in 1989. When that revolutionary year ended the bells tolled for the victory of the people over oppression and the dead hand of rigid planning. For the first time in Europe's history, governments working towards liberty, pluralist representative democracy, and the self-determination of subject nations were in prospect from the Atlantic to the Urals.

It is true that the quality of democracy is variable. Most of the former Eastern bloc countries need time to develop the structures and habits of democratic life. But there are models of good practice, such as the Scandinavian countries, The Netherlands, Switzerland and many others. The Federal Republic of (West)

Germany and Spain are also now democracies which have successfully brought power closer to the people through the creation of autonomous states or regions within an overall political and economic framework. It is noteworthy that both of these examples were formerly totalitarian dictatorships. Such is the scope for successful reform, and such is the inspiration for Central and Eastern Europe's new democracies.

On the other hand France, the pioneer of revolution in Europe, and Britain, with its 'mother of parliaments', are increasingly perceived to be among Europe's most centralised and authoritarian states.

With the common cause of democracy established and a growing recognition of the value of diversity, the scene is set for the creation of a supra-national infrastructure to draw Europe into a unified commonwealth. Much of the groundwork has already been done. But integrating hitherto irreconcilable political, military and economic structures into a truly united Europe will be a delicate task, requiring skilful and visionary statesmanship.

The signalled non-intervention of the Red Army in the internal affairs of the Soviet satellite countries enabled the democratisation of those countries to proceed. So will arms reductions on both sides create the trust and the space for the emergence of a new political and economic order, capable of bridging the historic divide. The catalyst is unified Germany.

The Germans are the only ethnic group with a substantial population on both sides of the former 'Iron Curtain'. The opening of the Berlin Wall in 1989 made unification of both Germanies inevitable. To allay fears of a resurgent German imperialism, it was necessary for the two parts of Germany to reduce the presence of military forces. The subsequent 'peace dividend', through further reducing military power Europe-wide, offers the prospect of a peaceful and prosperous united Europe.

Germany embodies a very important characteristic which enhances its catalytic role. The prosperous West Germany became the model for the unified Germany, whose democratic decentralised federal structure now forms a group of 15 autonomous states or *Länder*, all operating within a unified economic and monetary framework. As has been indicated in the main text, the actual number of *Länder* may change but the federal structure will remain. Such an arrangement clearly has applicability in the wider European context.

A further element is the Deutschmark, already Europe's strongest currency. Unification will in due course further strengthen the Deutschmark as both the common German currency, and the main financial vehicle for funding much needed investment in the former Soviet satellites. By the end of the century it is likely that the Deutschmark will be the dominant component of a common European currency. Although each country will be able to issue currency of local design, European monetary union is likely to be achieved in effect through the Europeanisation of the Deutschmark.

The creation of a pan-European supra-national political and economic infrastructure will almost certainly be founded upon the existing European Community (EC). The EC already embraces about half of Europe's population, and by far the most prosperous half. Closely associated with the EC is the European Free Trade Association (EFTA), a group of smaller Western states who have been thus far unwilling to sacrifice either neutrality or the measure of national sovereignty required for entry to the EC. Co-operation between the EC and EFTA has, however, created the framework for a 'European Economic Area' (EEA) with freedom of movement of goods, services, capital and people.

The next step is the application by the former Communist countries of Central and Eastern Europe for a similar associate status with the EC, and even full membership. What is beginning to emerge, if perhaps on a temporary basis, is a club with different categories of membership. Full membership, which requires full acceptance of the disciplines and obligations of the EC, gives voting rights and therefore influence over the institution's development. Lesser categories of membership give access to markets and other benefits, but with limited influence on EC rule-setting. It will be most important for the equitable development of a properly pan-European structure to have fair mechanisms to enable movement between membership categories.

As all this evolves, it is certain that a number of functions formerly carried out by nation states will in future be the responsibility of the supra-national institutions. This is increasingly the case for existing EC members. These functions will include setting and policing rules of interstate trade, standards, competition, control of common currency and monetary systems, external tariffs, and probably a military dimension.

At the same time, as the stateless nations and other national, cultural and linguistic minorities secure autonomy, or independence, so will many functions formerly carried out by the large nation states be taken over by new more localised autonomous or independent governments. These functions may vary from case to case but may typically include economic development, roads and transport, communications media, education, health, social provision, cultural and linguistic developments.

If such functions are transferred in this way, upwards to European level, or downwards to small nation level, does this mean the disappearance from the political map of the larger nation states such as France, Britain, Germany or Spain? Perhaps, but it is more likely that a middle tier will remain as associations of nations with the task of representing and coordinating major issues affecting their members. These 'mega regions' or clubs would be ideal vehicles to act as standing committees of, and electoral colleges to select representatives for, the enlarged European parliament — an important role, bearing in mind that the parliament will have political responsibility for a territory providing home for some 670,000,000 people — almost three times the population of the USA.

The exact disposition of these mega regions or remnant large nation states within the overall European framework will be subject to the evolution of the supra-national infrastructure. The groupings of nations set out in the foregoing pages of this book, such as Scandinavia, British Isles, Low Countries, and so on, illustrate a possible starting point. Some interesting variations do, however, present themselves. It has been suggested for example that the Baltic states could associate with Scandinavia to form a Balto-Scandinavian confederation. It is possible to visualise Hungary and the Catholic western Yugoslavs linking up with Austria, leaving the remaining Orthodox Balkan lands to form a separate association with Greece. A political grouping reflecting the cultural bond between the countries of the Celtic League offers another future possibility.

While the development of a supra-national infrastructure and of mega regions, along the lines described above, offers a possible framework for the eventual creation of a viable 'three tier' united Europe, it is the hundred nations themselves which will increasingly address the everyday needs of their citizens. This will allow the smaller nations more equitable participation in a pan-European future than ever previously conceived. A healthy characteristic of the new Europe is that henceforth all nations and language communities, even the largest, will be minorities.

The struggle of the stateless nations to achieve self-determination is a fundamental part of the struggle for democracy itself. Satisfactory progress of this struggle will be one of the most rewarding aspects of building the new Europe. Of course the transfer of power from large states to re-emerging nations is not automatic: an inertia of economic dominance and territorial prestige on the part of the former imperial states must be overcome. But great strength flows from the moral weight of a just cause backed by a well organised and internationally supported campaign. This book indicates where action of this kind is likely to take place.

As the American philosopher Henry D. Thoreau said: 'greater than the power of mighty armies is the force of an idea whose time has come'.

The time for creating 'one Europe of a hundred nations' is now truly upon us. The task is the greatest, most worthy and exciting adventure of our generation. If we rise to it, our children will surely inherit a humane, peaceful and prosperous European Commonwealth in which pride of language and culture is balanced by respect for the richness of European diversity.

Appendix 1 – THE FAMILY TREE OF EUROPE'S LANGUAGES

Europe's languages are classified into families and branches. The map (not to scale) shows the distribution of the main language families. The table below sets out all of the languages and their family relationships.

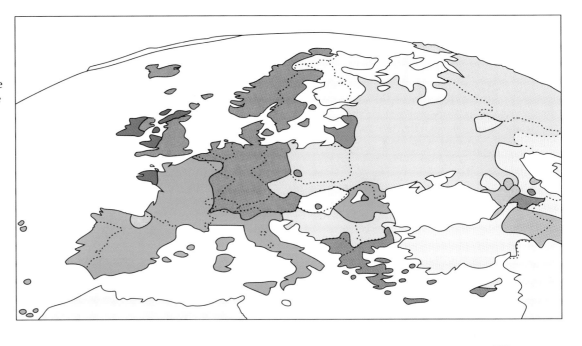

☐ Basque & Caucasian	■ Celtic	☐ Uralic	■ Indo-Iranian	■ Germanic	☐ Slavic	☐ Turkic
■ Greek,Albanian,Armenian	■ Romance	■ Baltic	☐ Semitic			

THE BASQUE FAMILY –
Basque

THE CAUCASIAN FAMILY –

Kartvelian branch: Georgian, Adzar, Mingrelian, Svanetian, Laz

Nakh (Veinakh) branch: Chechen, Ingush

Dagestan branch: Avar, Lak, Dargwa, Tabasaram, Lezghi, Agul, Rutvl, Tsakhur, Khinalug, Budukh, Kryz, Udi

Ardyge-Abkhaz branch: Adyge, Kabarda, Circassian, Abkhaz, Abazin

THE INDO-EUROPEAN FAMILY –

Indo-Iranian branch: Kurdish, Romany, Ossetin, Tat, Talysh

Albanian branch: Albanian

Armenian branch: Armenian

Greek branch: Greek

Celtic branch: Welsh, Cornish, Breton, Irish, Scots Gaelic, Manx

Italic branch: Latin, Portuguese, Gallego, Spanish, Yanito, Canarian, Catalan, Occitan, Franco-Provençal, French, Walloon, Romansch, Ladino, Friulan, Sard, Corsican, Italian, Romanian

Baltic branch: Lithuanian, Latvian

Slavic branch: Russian, Ukrainian, Belorussian, Czech, Slovak, Polish, Kashubian, Sorbian, Slovene, Serb, Croat, Macedonian, Bulgarian

Germanic branch: High German, Low German, Yiddish, Dutch, Flemish, Frisian, Scots, English, Icelandic, Faroese, Norwegian, Swedish, Danish

THE URALIC FAMILY –

Finnic branch: Finnish, Estonian, Karelian, Sami, Komi, Mari, Mordvin, Udmurt

Ugric branch: Hungarian

Samoyedic branch: Samoyed

THE SEMITIC FAMILY –
Arabic, Maltese

THE ALTALC FAMILY –

Turkic branch: Turkish, Azeri, Kumyk, Nogay, Tatar, Karachay, Balkar, Chuvash, Gaganz

Mongol branch: Kalmyk

THE INUIT-ALEUT FAMILY –
Greenlandic

Appendix 2 – EUROPE'S RELIGIOUS SPECTRUM

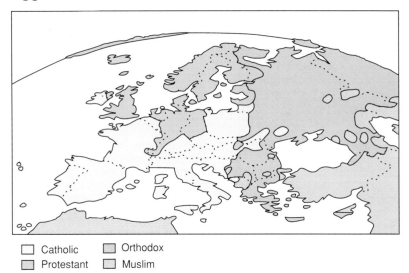

☐ Catholic	☐ Orthodox
☐ Protestant	☐ Muslim

In the Middle Ages Europe and Christendom were essentially one and the same, moulded by two great traditions — Catholicism in the West and Orthodoxy in the East. With the Reformation, the Protestant churches were to form a third major influence on the development of European spiritual thought. Although Islam has tended to be peripheral, it has through the centuries greatly affected Europe's political development.

The map (not to scale) shows the long-standing areas of influence of each of these major creeds.

Appendix 3 – THE PERSISTENCE OF MONARCHY

Despite the evolution of widely held egalitarian concepts of democracy, ten constitutional monarchies continue to exist in Europe. An anachronism perhaps, but these crowned heads, who nowadays have little, if any, real political power, enjoy surprising levels of popular affection. They are listed as follows:

Denmark	Queen Margaret	accession 1972
Norway	King Olav V	1957
Sweden	King Carl XVI Gustaf	1973
Britain (UK)	Queen Elizabeth	1953
Netherlands	Queen Beatrix	1980
Belgium	King Baudouin	1951
Luxemburg	Grand Duke Prince Jean	1964
Monaco	Prince Rainier III	1949
Spain	King Juan Carlos	1975
Liechtenstein	Prince Hans Adam	1989

Of these current monarchies, Spain's was reinstated as recently as 1975 after 44 years' absence. Among Europe's other former monarchies too, claimants to dissolved thrones wait and hope for the restoration of their crowns. A search for identity in the West and the revolution in Eastern Europe have given rise to a flurry of activity among royal hopefuls offering themselves to the service of their countries as follows:

France	dissolved	1870	Henri, Count of Paris
Portugal		1910	Edward, Duke of Braganza
Germany / Prussia		1918	Prince Louis Ferdinand
Italy		1946	Prince Victor Emmanuel
Austria / Hungary		1919	Otto von Habsburg
Serbia / Yugoslavia		1941	Crown Prince Alexander
Montenegro		1921	King Nikola II
Greece		1967	King Constantine II
Albania		1939	King Leka
Bulgaria		1946	King Simeon II
Romania		1948	King Michael
Russia		1918	Grand Duke Vladimir

Claimants also exist for vacant thrones in a number of former German and Italian principalities. The chance of successful reinstatement of any of these, or the above former monarchies, is a matter for conjecture, but is by no means ruled out.

Appendix 4 – 1989 – THE YEAR OF REVOLUTION

In one amazing year 'people power' toppled the apparently vice-like control of totalitarian Communist governments in Eastern Europe. At the beginning of the year possibilities for change were in the air. Hitherto the pace had been slow, but as the months of 1989 passed, the world watched on television as events moved faster and faster to reach their breathtaking Christmas climax. These events are summarised below:

January
The 'Iron Curtain' is still in place, with Communist governments throughout Eastern Europe. In the USSR, Hungary, Poland and Yugoslavia, however, discussion of democratic ideas is increasingly tolerated. Soviet leader, Mikhail Gorbachev announces that the Communist Party is no longer guaranteed a leading role.

February
In Poland the Communist government extends formal round-table discussions to the independent trade union Solidarity and the Catholic Church. Czechoslovak dissident Vaclav Havel is arrested for incitement and given a nine-month sentence.

March
After mass demonstrations for freedom and democracy, the Hungarian government promises reform and re-adopts the pre-Communist national coat of arms. The Baltic republic re-adopt their pre-Communist flags. The first partially free elections for the people's congress take place in the USSR.

April
The Polish government agrees to the legalisation of Solidarity and to democratic elections. 30 peaceful nationalist demonstrators killed by Soviet troops in Tbilisi, Georgia.

May
The Hungarian government opens the 'Iron Curtain' by destroying its border fence with Austria.

June
Solidarity wins an overwhelming majority in the Polish parliamentary elections.

July
20,000 demonstrate in Kishinev, the Soviet Moldavian capital, for Moldavian language rights.

August
Tadeusz Mazowiecki becomes the first prime minister of a non-Communist Polish government in over 40 years. A 500 mile human chain is staged in the Baltic states in protest against Soviet domination. Romanian replaces Russian as the official language of Moldavia.

September
Hungary agrees to democratic rule and opens its border to allow East Germans to cross to the West without visas. A new Slovene constitution guarantees the right to secede from Yugoslavia.

October
A mass exodus to the West of East German citizens through the open Austro-Hungarian border swells. The East German Communist government collapses following anti-government demonstrations in Leipzig. Hungarians celebrate the promise of free elections and representative democracy. Gennady Gerasimov, of the Soviet Foreign Ministry, announces the 'Frank Sinatra Doctrine' guaranteeing the right of former Soviet satellites freedom to choose their own destiny.

November
The East German government opens the Berlin wall and promises free elections amid popular euphoria. Bulgaria's Communist leader Todor Zhivkov is ousted. In Czechoslovakia the Communist government gives up power in response to sustained peaceful pro-democracy demonstrations. Free democratic elections are promised for Czechoslovakia.

December
Soviet President Gorbachev meets the Pope and promises to guarantee religious liberty in the USSR. United States President Bush meets Gorbachev and both parties agree to large-scale arms reductions in Europe and to an end to the 'Cold War'. In Romania, after the government tries to crush a popular protest, the people, aided by the army, rise up and topple the hated regime of Nicolae Ceucescu after ten days of bitter fighting. Ceucescu is executed on Christmas Day and free elections are promised for Romania by the new provisional government. Vaclav Havel, freed from jail, becomes the non-Communist president of Czechoslovakia.

As the New Year bells toll and the Romanians clear up isolated pockets of resistance, the power monopoly of totalitarian Communism is broken. A future for democracy is in prospect throughout Europe, with, for a further short period, the single exception of backward Albania, Europe's last isolated bastion of Communist orthodoxy.

Appendix 5 – INDEPENDENCE BLOSSOMS

In the first nine decades of the 20th century no less than twenty formerly dependent European countries freed themselves from external domination to become, or regain the status of, independent nation states. Of that number, eight subsequently lost their independence due to incorporation within the Soviet Union. The following table lists both categories:

Country	Date, Free from	Date, lost to
Norway	1905, Sweden	
Bulgaria	1908, Turkey	
Albania	1913, Turkey	
Finland	1917, Russia	
Georgia	1917, Russia & Turkey	1921, USSR
Ukraine	1918, Russia & Austro-Hungary	1922, USSR
Lithuania	1918, Russia	1940, USSR
Estonia	1918, Russia	1940, USSR
Poland	1918, Germany, Russia & Austro-Hungary	
Latvia	1918, Russia	1940, USSR
Czechoslovakia	1918, Austro-Hungary	
Yugoslavia	1918, Austro-Hungary	
Armenia	1918, Russia & Turkey	1920, USSR
White Russia	1918, Russia	1922, USSR
Azerbaijan	1918, Russia	1920, USSR
Ireland	1919, Britain	
Vatican	1929, Italy	
Iceland	1944, Denmark	
Malta	1960, Britain	
Cyprus	1964, Britain	

Besides these and the ten, together with West Berlin, individual states (*Länder*) within post-Second World War West Germany, another ten national groups currently have partial autonomy. They were:

Åland, Canary Islands, Catalonia, Euskadi, Faroe Islands, Flanders, Galicia, Gibraltar, Greenland, Wallonia.

The revolutionary events of 1989 and the subsequent democratisation of Central and Eastern Europe set in motion a main of independence bids which led to the demise of the USSR and the break-up of Yugoslavia. The following table lists these reborn nations.

Country	Date	Free from	UN Recognition
Lithuania	1990	USSR	1991
Estonia	1990	USSR	1991
Slovenia	1990	Yugoslavia	1992
Georgia	1991	USSR	—
Croatia	1991	Yugoslavia	1992
Russia	1991	USSR	*1991
Latvia	1991	USSR	1991
Ukraine	1991	USSR	*1945
Belarus	1991	USSR	*1945
Moldova	1991	USSR	1992
Azerbaijan	1991	USSR	1992
Macedonia	1991	Yugoslavia	—
Armenia	1991	USSR	1992
Bosnia-Hercegovina	1991	Yugoslavia	—

* In 1991 Russia inherited the USSR's place on the UN security council. As an anomaly of the UN's formation, Ukraine and Belorussia (now Belarus) were recognised in 1945.

With German reunification in 1990, the former Communist German Democratic Republic disappeared. In its place five reconstituted *Länder* emerged, bringing the total within the new Germany to fifteen, plus a united Berlin. The reintroduction of democracy in neighbouring Czechoslovakia brought real autonomy to Slovakia. In the two years from the beginning of 1990 to the end of 1991, Europe's territorial make-up changed as follows:

	Jan 1990	Dec 1991
Independent states	35	47*
German *Länder* and Berlin	11	16
Autonomous territories	11	11

* includes Macedonia, Bosnia-Hercegovina and Georgia whose independent status was not confirmed.

SELECTED BIBLIOGRAPHY

The source material for *One Europe — 100 Nations* covers a vast range of books, pamphlets, manuscripts and personal notes in many languages. To give a complete list would be impractical but the following books and periodicals provide useful additional background.

BERRISFORD ELLIS, P. and MAC A'GHOBHAINN, S. (1971) *The Problem of Language Revival*. Inverness: Club Leabhar.

BROWN, A., FENNELL, J., KASER, M. and WILLETTS, H. T. (1982) *The Cambridge Encyclopedia of Russia and the Soviet Union*. Cambridge: Cambridge University Press.

CRYSTAL, D. (1988) *The Cambridge Encyclopedia of Language*. London: Guild Publishing.

EUROPA YEAR BOOK (1986) *A World Survey*. London: Europa Publications.

ELKINS, T. H. (1960) *Germany*. London: Christophers.

FOUERE Y. (1968) *L'Europe aux Cent Drapeaux*. Paris: Presses d'Europe.

LEGRAND, J. (1990) *Chronicle of the Year 1989*. London: Longman.

LOUDA, J. and MACLAGAN, M. (1981) *Lines of Succession*. London: Orbis.

NEUBECKER, O. (1977) *Heraldry Sources, Symbols and Meaning*. London: Macdonald.

O'DELL, A. C. (1957) *The Scandinavian World*. London: Longmans.

PEDERSEN, C. F. (1971) *The International Flag Book in Colour*. London: Blandford Press.

SHACKLETON, M. R. (1962) *Europe — A Regional Geography*. London: Longmans.

SMITH, W. (1975) *Flags Through the Ages and Across the World*. Maidenhead: McGraw-Hill.

STEPHENS, M. (1978) *Linguistic Minorities in Western Europe*. Llandysul: Gomer Press.

TREHARNE, R. F. and FULLARD, H. (1973) *Muir's Historical Atlas, Ancient, Medieval and Modern*. London: Geo. Philip.

VOLBORTH, C. A. VON (1973) *Heraldry of the World*. London: Blandford Press.

Western Europe 1989 – A Political and Economic Survey (1988) London: Europa Publications.

Useful Periodicals

Contact Bulletin (European Bureau for Lesser Used Languages, Dublin)
The Economist (London)
Europa de les Nacions (CIEMEN, Barcelona)
The European (London)
Financial Times (London)
The Flag Bulletin (Winchester, Mass., USA)